FOUR FRIDAYS

LESSONS LEARNED BY LETTING GO

CYNTHIA BARLOW

INGENIUM BOOKS

ISBNs

eBook 978-1-989059-51-7

Paperback 978-1-989059-50-0

Hard Cover 978-1-989059-52-4

Audiobook 978-1-989059-53-1

Author photo credit: Michelle Valberg, Valberg Imaging

PRAISE FOR FOUR FRIDAYS

"I read *Four Fridays* through tears of wonder—it is an unforgettable journey of illumination. You could not ask for a more astute witness to life and death than Cynthia Barlow."

TERRI CHENEY, AUTHOR OF NEW YORK
TIMES BESTSELLER *MANIC: A MEMOIR*

"Four Fridays is beautiful and elegantly written. A memoir of deep friendship, loss and love. A must read for every woman rising above their circumstances. 'I have found my place at the table, my voice.' Open, with raw honesty — a reflection of the depths of a life-long friendship."

STEPHANIE THORNTON PLYMALE,
BESTSELLING AUTHOR, *AMERICAN
DAUGHTER*

"A powerful read. I found myself laughing, crying, and flipping pages as fast as I could. The author succeeded in inserting much of her accumulated wisdom into the pages. This is a moving and compelling read. I highly recommend this book."

MAUREEN FISHER, AUTHOR, *FUR BALL
FEVER*

"What if you had a lifelong friend. And your friend was dying… and you knew that your time together was coming to an end. That you had four Fridays left. What would you reflect upon, laugh at, learn? This is the premise of *Four Fridays*. Anyone who has had a friend or lost a friend, anyone who's wondered about the mysteries of life or wrestled with the finality of death, will be taken in by this poignant, unexpectedly funny and soul stirring memoir."

"Loss. Sadness. Gratitude. Wonder. Delight. Words from *Four Fridays*. A beautifully written book. What makes this book so raw, real and captivating is that you can truly hear the author's voice—in each word, sentence, paragraph, through each chapter—and you can feel her emotions, see her struggles and watch her rise above as she ignites all her reader's senses.

What a gift! I didn't want to put this book down."

"*Four Fridays* is a vividly touching account of love and loss, hope and fear, and ultimately, of growth. Cynthia's shameless honesty, clever humour and profound humanity propels the reader through their own journey of self-discovery. An absolute gem!"

JOHN LARSEN, EVP EDELMAN, NATIONAL PRACTICE LEAD, CRISIS & RISK (CANADA) GLOBAL LEAD, CORONAVIRUS TASK FORCE

"Having worked and lived in a large funeral home during college, I felt I knew a lot about death and grieving. What I didn't know anything about was dying and being with someone who is. I'm clear that we'll all wind up dead one day. What I don't want is for anyone I care about to go there alone. This book has had me realize that I could actually develop the courage, caring and sense of humor to be present with someone who is slipping away, and perhaps thereby increase the odds that others will be there for me as well."

DAN HAYGEMAN, INTERNATIONAL EFFECTIVENESS COACH

"An inspiring reflection of true friendship and a powerful reminder to pay attention to the time you have with those you love. In today's restless society, *Four Fridays* provides a stark reminder to relish the moment and not take the small things for granted. An amazing book!"

LOUIS GOLDBERG, PRES., VOLITIONU

CONTENTS

For Joy
and her Mexican momma, may she rest in peace

1

STILL THE SAME?

She looks the same, but she's not.

As I exit the air-conditioned airport terminal, it feels like I've walked straight into the huge exhaust pipe of an enormous drier. A wall of hot. Sticky hot. Immediate hot. Perspiration forms on my forehead within seconds.

I have arrived in sunny Puerto Vallarta, Mexico, land of expats and tourists, creative types, and freedom seekers, to spend two weeks with my dear friend, Christina. The season is over and only a few idle tourists now roam the streets; those who, like Christina, live here year-round. The airport is practically empty midweek in mid-May, a month I've not been here before.

All around me, everything looks and sounds same. Everything. It all looks and sounds exactly like the tender memories I hold in my mind. The crisp navy blue of the uniformed police officers. The local luxuries and basic necessities for sale in tiny *tiendas*. The chattering of the people speaking their native tongue unbelievably quickly, Spanish words bursting from their mouths like strings of small firecrackers. All of it is familiar. I have been here dozens of times. And all of it looks and sounds just as I remember it, but it *feels* different this trip. It is a paradox, to feel comforted yet disconcerted simultaneously.

Christina pulls up in her trusty, dusty, old warrior of a car. Her fine blond hair is still short, her body sturdy and strong. Her smile is still broad and sincere, her laugh lively and engaging. Her blue eyes still twinkle. She is tan in the way those who live in southern sunshine become over the years, the warm caramel color of her skin baked in like a ginger cookie pulled straight from the oven. She wears a flowing sleeveless dress. There are, as always, brightly beaded, indigenous dangle earrings hanging from her ears that shimmy when she moves. As she hops from the car and walks toward me, she looks exactly the same. But she's not.

We hug, kiss, throw the bags in the back, jump inside the air-conditioned metal beast for some fast relief, and we're off. We're headed to one of her favorite Italian restaurants after a few errands. There are always errands when traveling with Christina. It's never a straight line from here to there, from where we are to where we're going. There are always frequent stops along the way, both planned and unplanned. She knows a lot of people, having lived here for fifteen years, and bumps into them while running errands, which doubles the time it takes to complete any planned tasks. She usually isn't governed by time — I fall prey to that tendency far more than she — but now, time is her most precious commodity, so she is beginning to guard it carefully.

The longer she's in Boca, the less she likes coming into the city, she says. She tries to keep it to once a week these days. She and her friend and fellow Boca resident, Leo, often drive to town together, or alternate for trips to Costco, the main reason for the weekly jaunts. Costco is king in that town, at least among the expats, and it's air-conditioned, always a plus. This trip, the errands include a random drive-through window where she can pay the phone bill. Then the water bill. Then, she has an acupuncturist appointment, which is around the block from her favorite Italian restaurant, where we'll grab an early supper. Lastly, we'll hit Costco, and then, finally, home to Casa la Ventana in Boca de Tomatlán, fifteen kilometers south of Puerto Vallarta.

Casa la Ventana, her four-level, four-bedroom, open-air home rises halfway up from the side of the mountain on the south side of the river that cuts Boca in two. The *casa* demands to be noticed, daring you not to admire and stare at this majestic structure that clings to the side of a mountain, seeming to defy the laws of gravity and balance. Not only well-designed and constructed, it is also painted a bright orange which makes it visible from anywhere in the town on the north side of the river. Christina's early years as a retirement home consultant served her well as she prepared to build her own final resting place. *I built that place to die in it*, she would say. She and her husband (at the time), Don, took years to travel and research before choosing Boca as the spot they wanted to live out the rest of their years. Christina had a checklist: airport access, hospital and health care services, dollar value, land costs, and community life. She knew exactly what she was looking for. The sleepy little fishing village of a few hundred residents south of Puerto Vallarta was it. They found and bought a bit of property and began to build their forever home.

Christina became unhappy with the person they had hired to execute her vision, so she fired him and took over the task of managing the forty or so Mexican workmen it took to build *la casa* over the course of sixteen months. Her husband took a back seat in directing the crew, but he drank a few beers with them on a regular basis, and ran errands to help keep them working. It was a Herculean effort, but she knew what she was doing, and the results are on display in the myriad details she took into consideration—from the quality of construction and craftsmanship to the positioning of the windows, even in the showers, that provide stunning views of the mountains or glimpses of the gardens from the inside of the house—all of it was precisely planned.

Her house is just like her: sturdy and stately, elegant and efficient. *I'll have everything I need* she would say to me over a glass of wine when reflecting on her grand design and ultimate plan. *A view from my bed of the mountains beyond, on two sides,* she would say. *One day, I'll never need to leave Casa la Ventana.* She always smiled when she said that.

Looks like that day will arrive sooner than either of us expected.

I had been gazing out the window in my Toronto apartment two weeks prior when she called to tell me. It was a sunny Sunday in May, a quiet day, a day when winter's white death grip seemed far behind. The tree outside my window was bursting with fresh green shoots.

I had been awaiting Christina's scheduled call that morning. We generally call each other on Sunday mornings since there is less commotion in the background. Less people around and less busyness to Boca's audible backdrop, though the roosters can be heard intermittently, always. It's impossible to shut the sounds of life out from the background of any kind of verbal communication in Boca de Tomatlán. The stray dogs won't be silenced, nor the children controlled, nor the roosters contained. The barking, laughing, crowing . . . they are constants.

I was somewhat disappointed when my phone rang and not the Skype window I had open and waiting; I like seeing her face. Later, I understood. She didn't want to be seen, not for this call.

After initial greetings, an *okay, who wants to go first?* kind of moment, Christina said, "You go."

"Sure," I said, delighted. I had spent several months examining my upcoming membership in the Social Security Club of the United States of America. There's a special membership qualification—you gotta be old. At least chronologically. Emotionally, Christina and I both think we shouldn't be members at all since we're only thirty-six years old in our heads. But, with that social security benefit date looming on the horizon, even as my energy level and enthusiasm for conducting multi-day leadership programs diminished, I figured it was time for an exit strategy that started with what I really wanted, instead of what might be practical or realistic or assumed by others.

I'm one of those people who was always so busy trying to survive in my thirties and forties that thoughts of retirement didn't occur to me until my fifties, and then only in some abstract fashion. It was something large and ominous, an *unknown* out there, in the future, far away. But now, retirement, or whatever that meant, was about to become a more concrete concept.

I pursued all kinds of options once I determined what funds could be expected from the various sources available to me. I spent a delightful number of hours designing a mobile retirement home out of an old school bus. Something creative and fun. Mental masturbation. I considered returning to the States to be closer to my sons and my grandchildren, who live in Baltimore, Maryland.

Peyton, my younger son's first child, now three, has rendered me irredeemably besotted. Madelyn, who followed two years later, put me over the edge. Unlike parenting, the joy of grandparenting is everything it's cracked up to be. With parenting comes all the crap. Responsibilities. Homework, health concerns, and sleepless nights. Not so with grandparenting. It's all fun and games if you let yourself get down on the floor and roll with them, which I do. But grandkids grow up and I rather like being the out-of-town fairy grandmother who swoops in for a week here and there and then flies away —back to my solitude and quiet.

After many months of weighing and considering, it came to me one day that I already knew exactly what I wanted; some place in or around Puerto Vallarta in the winters, and summers on the shores of the St. Lawrence River at my family cottage. I would grow old(er) with my BFF, Christina! Why was I even thinking about a stupid school bus? Motors? Moving parts? Honking big tires? No way. Christina and I had discussed this option of living together in our elder years some time back. She had toyed with the idea of selling Casa la Ventana and moving to a boat-only-access town where we'd share a space. But it was too early in the retirement process for either of us at that time. Yet, the thought sat imbedded like a sesame seed wedged under my gum, and I continued to feel its existence, a reminder of one possible future.

I shared all this with Christina, chattering away. I was excited. I had a three-year plan. The winter of 2021 I would be in PV, if not Boca. I would find a place, a long-term lease at a reasonable price, and begin my last act. Whatever that was. The one that would start with whatever retirement was supposed to look like. My mother didn't retire from teaching at a U.S. university until she was eighty-five, for heaven's sake! I had no idea what retirement was supposed to look like. I figured maybe I was already halfway there in that I don't work as much, and what work I do is by choice. That said, money was still a requirement and retirement benefits hadn't kicked in yet. And I wasn't ready to close it all down. I wasn't even sure if I would. Part of my vision included continuing coaching, which I find remarkably rewarding, and a surprising thing for a woman accustomed to group presentations and a stage.

"So, what's going on with you?" I finally asked, indicating it was now her turn to paint as equally a rosy picture of her tomorrows as I had just painted of mine. "What's new in Boca?" I was anticipating a chronicle of her daily life, the mini-dramas and small amusements, a catch-up coffee with a great girlfriend. But that's not the way it went. This call had nothing to do with catching up —except that it did.

"Well," Christina started, and then paused. She has several distinctly different *wells*. There's the one that starts a summation, an end to the discussion, which means that what is to follow is a *here's the bottom-line* decision. That one is short and uttered with a downstroke in tone, a period at the end of it. Another *well* is the more lilting, drawn out *w-e-l-l* . . . that ends on an upswing in tone. It indicates a selection of forthcoming options: we could do this, or that, or the other thing. . . . And then there's the softer, more even toned *well* which is followed by a compassionate reflection of truth, a gloved fist holding a scalpel. This was the *well* she had just uttered.

In her pause, thoughts flitted across my mind like skipping stones. Why was this the compassionate *well*? Was it the gloved fist? Was it the sadness? She only uses it when she's come to a conclusion that she feels compelled to share with someone because she needs to say it or they need to hear it. Or maybe there had been more drama with Don, or another family member? She had shared some recent hurtful events in past calls, and so with that kind of *well* I thought maybe she was heading in that direction. But I was wrong.

"The cancer's back," she said calmly. No embellishment. A scalpel slice. Swift. I didn't even feel the cut. She let it sink in before the blood began to flow. And I knew, before she told me the story, before she said anything else, I knew that this was it. I would not grow old with my friend.

This. Was. It.

I could feel it. In my heart and my gut. And I could hear it in Christina's voice.

"Stage four metastatic bone cancer. I have tumors growing on my spine."

Christina took a breath and released it, the way you do after you've answered a question you've been afraid of hearing but answered with the truth even though it hurt the recipient. It was the sound of unburdening oneself of a point of pain. "Probably other places, too." Her voice became smaller. This was hard for her to say, and she knew this was hard for me to hear, so close at heart, so far away, difficult to say out loud, to freeze the diagnosis, permanently, with words.

"Oh, Christina . . ." What could I say? I needed to *say* something. I needed to say *something*. I felt foolish for going on and on about some imaginary intertwined future together and I told her so. "Why didn't you stop me?" My throat tightened. "I . . . I . . . ." There were no words. They wouldn't come.

"Why would I stop you?" Her voice was calm and steady and sure and kind. I could tell she was smiling. "It's a pretty picture of a future you want. Just because I won't be there doesn't mean you can't still have it."

But it won't be the same, I thought but didn't say. How could it be the same? A future without Christina in it? A switch flipped inside me. I felt it. The professional switch. I would *feel* later. *Bracket that shit and put it aside.* Right then, I wanted information. Data. Details.

I found my voice. "Tell me. Just . . . tell me all of it."

Over the course of the next few minutes, Christina unfolded the story. I listened in stoic silence. She gave me an overview, the critical path of the previous three months, things she'd not told me as she was going through them: finding a weird bump on her clavicle that led to a doctor visit in Feb; the PET scan in Guadalajara and subsequent operation in March; the resulting diagnosis of metastatic stage four bone cancer.

The timeline emerged more clearly as she spoke, and I realized she'd waited a long time to tell me this. I noticed the green ooze of envy as it seeped under the doorjamb of my professional listening skills. How could she not have told me before this? How many others knew before me? Later, in an oblique way, it became clear that she worked her way from tertiary to primary relationships, as though moving from the outer rings of a target toward the bullseye. From necessary and professional, to difficult and personal. She had told Nate, her son and only child, only days before.

"How long?" I wanted to know *time.* Goddamn time.

"The stats say 20 percent of those who seek treatment live up to five years."

"Treatment meaning chemo and radiation, right?"

"Yes." She paused, scalpel in hand. "I've decided not to seek treatment." This was Christina's third rodeo and she was choosing not to get on the chemo horse again. Her first battle began with breast cancer fifteen years ago. She was fierce in her attack. Full on. Lost her hair but saved her breasts; they carry the scars of radiation burns. When she was ten years cancer-free, we popped a bottle of champagne and celebrated her full victory.

Only a year later, the insidious enemy resurfaced and so she strapped on her armor again. At that time, she told the doctors that if they found enemy troops in her lymph nodes to simply sew her back up and send her home. But they didn't, and she limped away from that battle. After treatment the doctors declared her okay, but a year after that, she told me that she just didn't feel herself, that she was sure it was still in her body. She was right. This time, she didn't have the energy nor appetite to ride into battle again. Her armor had rusted over and it no longer fit. She wanted to feel well and with it until she couldn't.

"I'm choosing quality over quantity. The effects of chemo, the throwing up, I won't do it again. I won't." There was a determination in her voice I recognized well. "I don't want to be sick from now until I die."

She wanted mental clarity. She wanted emotional completion. I understood that, but I recoiled internally when she uttered the word *die*. The silence sat for a second. When she spoke next, she'd softened. There was a touch of wistfulness, something I rarely heard in her voice. It implied regret, and she only carried one that I know of. Christina pretty much laughs things off or thinks them through and then cleans them up.

"I always knew I'd die in Casa la Ventana," she said. "I just didn't think it'd be this soon." And then, more silence. I heard her sigh. A small sigh.

I was glad for the lack of video, glad not to see her face while listening to her speak. I felt as though a sink hole had opened up in the floor beneath me, the foundation of a familiar future ripped away, rendered irrelevant. I could not, while she spoke, imagine a future void of her voice. Her strength was a given, her invincibility assumed. At least, by me, and I suspect, everyone who knew her. Thank God I wasn't looking at her; it would have been too much.

"How are you really? How's the pain?" I wanted details. As though by knowing them I could somehow pull her closer.

"It's okay. Comes and goes. At this point, it's the drop in my energy level I notice most." She reminded me that years before, she and Leo and some friends had been out in his boat when they hit some rough waves. Christina had come down off her seat and onto the floor of the boat, landing hard on her coccyx and compressing a disc. The pain would come and go, depending on her physical exertion, and she had grown used to its intermittent interruptions to her lifestyle. There were often times when her back would ache enough to postpone whatever activity we had planned that particular day. So, when her lower back pain increased in both regularity and intensity over the course of the past year, she delayed seeking a doctor's examination, thinking the pain from the tumors growing along her spine was merely old pain from the disc damage. When it became chronic pain in January 2018, she told me later, she knew. Before she even scheduled the doctor appointment in February, she knew the cancer was back. She knew, but she didn't want to know.

I don't even remember everything she shared that day. I'm sure I was in a bit of shock, at least emotionally. All I knew was that I was too far away, and we had too little time.

"When can I come visit you?" I said. The news had altered my personal priority pole. *Time.* I wanted to see her as soon as possible, while she was still mobile.

"*W-e-l-l,*" she began, and I smiled. It was the upbeat *well,* the good *well,* and I knew she had already considered the options I was about to hear. I went online while she spoke and searched for available flights. By the time we hung up the phone, there was a plan in place: one-on-one girlfriend time in ten days for two whole weeks.

It will be time to pretend she's still the same.

Christina will leave this earth the same way and from the same form of cancer that took another dear friend of mine, Alan Mirabelli. He died in December 2017. Metastatic bone cancer, stage four. His started in his throat, hers in her breast. His tumors attached themselves to his femur and tibia, hers to her spine and skull. He also chose quality of existence over quantity of days.

Alan and I met twenty-five years ago when he attended several programs I conducted. We grew to love and respect each other deeply. He lived in Ottawa and I in Toronto, and we would have long conversations by phone. He was with it and active—though in a reduced capacity—until about a week before he died. I visited him each month but walked the path with him emotionally on a daily basis. It was a rewarding and joyful journey to pretend that I, too, had been told I had only nine months to live. It enhanced my own appreciation for the smaller delights of life, things like breathing, and walking, and seeing, and talking. You know, all those little things we take for granted until they're taken away, until the threat of their impending departure awakens us to their delights. Things like the way a flower sways in the breeze or water winds its way across the stony stream that runs along his back patio. I paid close attention to the nuances of life for that nine-month marathon with Alan. It was enlivening.

And then he died, dammit. Three days before Christmas. I spoke at his funeral in January. After that, I stopped paying attention to life. Just shut down. The grey, cold days and nights of February left me tired and listless. I stopped playing the game—that I had a stale date like Alan—and stopped noticing any daily delights. I stopped taking pleasure in being alive, mostly because I fell ill for the entire month of February. I laid on my couch and coughed for a month. I suspect the loss of attention, the retreat from life, invited the illness in.

And now, to walk that path with a loved one again, so soon, feels *too* soon. And though I feel I've been prepared for this additional journey—even had a dress rehearsal with Alan—I do *not* want to participate in this show with Christina. Opening night can wait.

But I *will* make this journey with her. Somehow. Whatever comes, I vow to myself, I will be present and aware for this precious goodbye. I will not waste what time she might have left on this earth with withering thoughts of what might have been in some fantasy future. I will be present. I will notice details again. I will rejoice in her life. I will rejoice in my life and its remaining delights. I will rejoice in *life*, period.

And I will fucking start paying attention again.

2

THE BEGINNING OF BUDDIES

Christina and I met in 1988, in the comfortable northern suburbs of Baltimore, Maryland. It was a time of shoulder pads and big hair and legwarmers. A time of women breaking through (some) glass ceilings and into levels of leadership that had hitherto been out of reach. A time when Christina was recovering from an abusive relationship while I was still in one. I liked and trusted her from the beginning and came to lean on her strength and wisdom.

Originally from Idaho, she had studied gerontology in college and now served as a consultant for high-end retirement communities. She was hired by various companies to help design, develop, and market an environment in which the elderly could both function and find fulfillment, a knowledge base that served her well when it came time to do the same for herself while building Casa la Ventana. She made a good living. Typically, the contracts were for two years, but the company who had hired her in Baltimore kept her on for four years, allowing our friendship time to grow meaningful, sustainable roots.

I remember the moment we first met. I was visiting a friend late one afternoon. Her son and mine liked to play together and Christina lived in the same townhouse complex. Returning home at the end of a work day, dressed in a shoulder-padded suit and high heels, the very picture of a businesswoman, she drove into a parking spot near where my friend and I—both dressed in crap compared to the elegant figure Christina cut—sat watching our boys chase each other around the common area. As Christina exited her car, my friend called out to her to join us for a glass of wine. Christina laughed and sauntered over. "Sounds great!" she said.

A fraction over five-foot-ten but with a physical energetic presence that made her seem six-foot-three, she looked like the poster child for the Nordic race with startling blonde hair and sparkling blue eyes. She had strong arms and hands, hands that knew livestock and plants, hands happy to dig in the dirt, a reflection of her childhood spent working the family farm. She came right over and joined us in the front yard, kicked off her shoes and wiggled her toes in the grass. Hitching up her skirt, she squatted down to sit on the front stoop. I liked that, the natural, unselfconsciousness of her transition from businesswoman to real folk like my friend and me in our endof-a-long-day-watching-kids clothing. No, *Oh, let me change and I'll be right back*. She transitioned right there, in front of us. I remember noticing and liking that she did that. I remember her smile, too, and how easily and freely she laughed.

Here's what I remember most: I wanted to get to know her. She had an inviting energy about her and a way of encircling people in unseen arms, bringing them together, and lifting them up. And I wanted to be lifted up. I wanted to feel on the inside as free and powerful as she appeared to be on the outside.

We made plans to see each other again. And we did, often, beginning with a lunch here or there and then a dinner, and phone calls, and movies, always replete with laughter and talks of the future. She was a working, single mom at the time, with a ten-year-old son, and I was a stay-at-home mom with two younger boys. But our values and dreams bound us together, creating all sorts of mysterious corners around which to peek, wormholes of what-ifs, with nooks and crannies of constant surprise and delight.

Now, those conversations about the future have an enforceable expiration date, the focus narrowed to the short-term, to today, this week, the next year. This year. The last of her life.

After we finish all her errands, Christina drives us to her favorite Italian restaurant; we'll hit Costco after we eat. We are the only customers. *Not a terribly reassuring review of the cuisine*, I think to myself, but then it is only 4:30 p.m., and just a wee bit early for the dinner rush. A gentleman appears from behind a curtain that leads to the kitchen. Seeing Christina, his face erupts in a broad smile.

"Ah, Christina! Bienvenidos! Como esta?"

"Bien, bien, gracias, Mario." Christina smiles in return and gives him a hug.

They chatter away in Spanish while he shows us to a table. The place is air-conditioned, reviving our spirits. We order today's house special, a freshly caught grouper atop a pile of pasta, and some sparkling water. Christina orders a glass of red wine. I join her. Mario pours us each a glass and, beaming, brings them to our table, one in each hand. He smiles just a teensy bit too broadly.

There is a sense of desperation in his warmth towards Christina. Too eager to please. It becomes apparent that he, too, knows of her diagnosis. And he, too, will most likely miss her, as will most everyone who's known her.

But she isn't anyone else's big sister, just mine. As the eldest of six children, I have never known what it's like to have a big sister or big brother to look up to. Christina is four years older than me, and I admired her so much so early on in our relationship that she became my spiritual big sister. I adopted her as such and she allowed it — welcomed it even. She was the youngest in her family and a big sister to no one.

She picks up her glass and raises it. "A toast," she says.

I raise my glass too. "You or me?"

"Me. I don't have that many left!" She laughs.

"No! Don't say that. You've got plenty left." A lie, we both know she doesn't.

Christina clucks her tongue and hushes me quiet. "To friendship," she says.

"To friendship," I repeat. "To ours."

We clink glasses. We are both dry-eyed because it's not real yet, not really. I've only just arrived a few hours ago, and here she sits, eating and talking and laughing, still sounding the same, still looking the same. And though I know intellectually that she is, in fact, dying, it doesn't feel that way in this moment of raised glasses. The time for tears feels far off in the future, the future about which we used to dream and talk and laugh.

Christina fills me in on all the town gossip and updates me on the lives of Boca's inhabitants while we eat our pasta and fish, languidly dipping our accompanying bread into olive oil, movements that belie my internal sense of urgency. This will be my last one-on-one visit with my big sister, my dear friend. I want to devour her and her laugh and her light and her love—her *life*— in the same way as I eat the pasta, somehow permanently digesting my friend into foreverness.

Christina grabs her handbag from the back of her chair, and signals Mario for the bill. We must be leaving. He places the flimsy slip of a receipt face down on the table and I reach for it, but she grabs it away.

"No. Mine. Your welcome dinner."

"But I was going to buy *you* dinner!"

"You can. Another time." I make a face of distasteful resignation. "Don't fight me on this," she says firmly. "Come to think of it, don't fight me on anything. Unless I ask you to."

"Fine. But we're going to Le Cliffe, okay? One night. We're gonna gaze at the sunset and have a beautiful meal. Just us. On me." I am as firm as she in my tone.

"Done."

"Good."

"Come on," she says, getting up from her chair. "Time to tackle Costco." And then she laughs. Again.

As we walk to the door I realize just how much I will miss her laugh.

3

WELCOME MEMORIES

Toto waits for us by the bridge with a couple of young boys who stand ready to start carting the car full of stuff Christina has purchased from Costco up to Casa la Ventana. I hop out of the car and give him a tight hug. I haven't seen him in three years. He's now twenty years old! I can hardly believe it. He was nine years old when we first met. I watched him grow up year to year. And now he's a man.

Toto and his girlfriend live in the downstairs room of the Cruz household, my former landlords, who live next door to Christina. Toto's mother, Silvia, the former matriarch, and someone I was deeply fond of, passed from stomach cancer two years ago. Toto was her last baby of five and she loved him with a fierce protection that spread the word among young men in town with less protective mothers. *Leave Toto out of any gang related activities else you gonna have a hard time with his momma.* Her efforts on his behalf show in the clear-eyed life he has created. Only five-foot-four or so, Toto is all big white smile and strong lean sinew. He runs up the stairs in front of me with my suitcase on his right shoulder as though he's skipping through a fairy forest, his calves undulating their way up the stairs. It's a walk in the park for him. Literally. Only, it's a park on the side of a mountain. With 101 steps.

I was never that healthy, I think, never that fit. But I know from previous experience that the daunting nature of the climb diminishes within a week or two of practice, which means that just about the time I can handle the stairs and view them as a friendly form of required exercise instead of punishment for a slovenly winter of constant chocolate consumption, it'll be time to head back home to the White Witch who invades Toronto each winter. Think Elsa from *Frozen*. But pissed off.

For the record, I hate cold weather. With a passion. I hate everything about it, dressing for it, walking through it, unwrapping myself afterward, trying to free myself like some living mummy, from layers and appendages— gloves, scarf, earmuffs, hat, boots, socks. It takes me ten minutes just to suit up whenever I leave my cozy, warm apartment, and at least another ten to unwind myself after returning home. It's exhausting and cumbersome. I was built for warm climes. My body works better, and it's a lot easier to slip on a pair of flip-flops than it is to strap on a pair of boots. The older I get, the more I like easy. These steps are not easy, but I am wearing flip-flops, which in my world, makes all things better.

The staircase was the first thing constructed, a necessary requirement when building anything into the side of a steep mountain. Gotta have a way to get people and materials *up*. It has two distinct sections. The first section —where a hand-painted wooden sign hangs on the side of the enormous beast of a retaining wall to the left, announcing this to be the entrance to Casa la Ventana— takes you from the path that runs along the river's edge to the pump house at the top of the stairs, or what *appears* to be the top. It is, in fact, only the halfway point, a daunting realization for the first-time visitor. Trust me, I know; I was literally heaving, unable to catch my breath, except to mutter, "Oh, gawd, there's more!" At the pump house, the staircase takes a 90-degree turn to the left and the second section of the staircase looms ahead, an equal number of steps awaiting the climber.

At that midway turning point—a brief reprieve—the house is in full view, as is the magnificent pool, patio, and *palapa* immediately to the left, giving a glimmer of hope to all us out-of-shape gringos accustomed to public transportation and escalators. That's where everyone (except Toto) stops and takes a few deep breaths. Between the pool and the house high above, Christina's magnificent gardens flourish in the moist, warm heat; resplendent greens and yellows and pinks and purples and reds and whites and oranges surround visitors. Additional boxed gardens run along the right-hand side of the stairs, bricked in square containers in which bloom all manner of exotic flora. Gazing skyward, three distinct staircase sections rise above and remain to be undertaken, each lifting the visitor to another level. Think of a third-floor walk-up with three standard size staircases. In a row. After the three you already climbed to get to the pump house. That's six flights! And Toto runs them all.

As I approach the last section of stairs that lead to the front door, gasping for breath, Maya greets me, her fluffy, fifteen-year-old husky tail wagging politely. It's the kind of wag she would give anybody walking up the stairs to her home. She's well-conditioned to an endless stream of visitors and Bed & Breakfast guests wandering the property. I met Maya eleven years ago but haven't seen her in three years, so polite is what I get. She plops down the top few steps toward me and I stop to greet her. She sniffs my knee and hand, looks up at me, and then her ears go back on her head, which in a Husky is the sign of acknowledgement and acquiescence, and she begins wiggling and whining in recognition. *Familiar human! Pack related! You're back!*

This show of genuine affection warms me deeply. There's nothing quite like being welcomed by an animal who doesn't have to love you but does anyway. It's sort of like being a grandparent: all the benefits and none of the responsibilities.

Bella, however, is a very different dog. Short-haired and small—maybe twenty-two pounds—she is a blur of black and white as she skitters across the terracotta tiles and out the front door. All claws and wiggles and small white teeth, she greets everyone she meets as a sort of rescuing angel. But Christina, well, Bella worships the woman who took her off the streets and into her home years ago. Christina is Bella's own personal goddess. The one who can do no wrong, ever. The one on whose bed she sleeps. She doesn't really relax unless Christina is home. Bella bolts straight down the stairs to Christina and then greets me warmly, but I'm no one special to her, unlike Maya who remembers me from many visits over many years.

Memory, I like it when it works in my favor.

Bruja, Christina's recent feline acquisition, is nowhere in sight. With silky black fur, she's like a long-legged mink. She and her feral friend, a grey tabby, showed up in the garden one day and Christina began leaving them leftovers on occasion. Bruja thought that was pretty nifty and decided to stay. Regular meals and Christina's bed were far superior options to the brush and its fearsome inhabitants: dogs, snakes, and scorpions. Her more wary companion chose to wander away. Bruja is a very smart cat who rolls with the punches. She's sleeping in the sun somewhere, I'm sure.

I slip back into Boca time in a single day, the sights and sounds of this tiny town evoking meaningful memories from the past. I learned about simplicity here, about the basics I take for granted, things like hot water, and showers, and electricity. I learned about the power of gratitude for the smallest of things, things like rain, and sunshine, and silence. The simple pleasures of life. Just by being back, I am reminded of those lessons and how far I've ebbed from some of them.

I wander along the dusty lower street (Boca only has two) that runs along the river's edge surveying what's popped up since my last visit three years ago. There is a new *lavandería* where you can drop off your pile of dirty clothes to be washed and returned to you, impeccably folded, smelling of mountain air, for sixty pesos. There is a liquor store and a new ice cream shop as well. They built a *malecon* two years ago and it really dresses up the place. But it's short, maybe sixty or seventy yards long, so it's not like you can walk it for very long. Puerta Vallarta's *malecon* runs for several kilometers providing ample opportunity to walk briskly—which I like to do—not stroll slowly which it seems most tourists enjoy. And the view from Boca's *malecon* is rather limited as well: fishing boats moored in the inlet where the river meets the ocean, and a couple of thatched *palapa* covered outdoor restaurants, though they can hardly be called restaurants. Tables and a small kitchen is more like it, but they roast up some mean fish with limited means. The *malecon* may have cleaned up the river's north shore, but it strikes me like a teenage girl playing grown-up by wearing a bra she doesn't yet need.

On the same road, the dusty unpaved one that runs along the river, sits Christina's *piece de resistance*, the clinic. It is a living legacy. With dental upstairs and medical below, it is a life-saving luxury now afforded the towns people and their mountain neighbors through Christina's determined pursuit of charitable donations from service organizations. For years she wooed donors and created alliances. She built awareness in the community. She got kids to go to the dentist. She would drive them into PV herself each week and buy them pizza afterwards at Costco. I recall a few dental trips with a car full of kids, singing songs together, their excitement about pizza palpable. We would have a tailgate party in Costco's parking lot, Christina smiling at *her kids* in the evening warmth. She even got the dentist to donate his services. Providing water purifiers, organizing trail-trash pick-ups, and beginning a scholarship program so that children could attend high school, are just a few of her contributions to the community, her impact on a wide number and variety of individuals too vast to fully realize.

She will be missed by many people, for many years. And some, like me, for the rest of our lives.

4

PURSUING PERMANENCE

One of the initial seeds for the strength of the friendship Christina and I grew over the years took root in a common understanding of certain concepts by which we chose to live.

Back in the seventies and eighties, the personal empowerment movement erupted on the West Coast. All kinds of *find yourself* classes emerged. The word *authentic* crept into the cultural consciousness, and then phrases like *live an authentic life, be true to yourself,* and *tell the truth.*

Christina had attended a series of courses while in Seattle, called The Excellence Series, which consisted of three multiday programs over the course of as many months. They were conducted by a human empowerment company called, at the time, Context Associated. Once in Baltimore, Christina aligned herself as a volunteer for that same company, who had recently opened an office in my hometown. The information Context espoused was hardly new, but their methodology, at least at the time, was unique. The main concepts—like accountability, responsibility, and full participation—

were presented in ways that made the concepts not only intellectually sound, but also able to be practiced and integrated easily and effectively. Emotionally moving, clarifying exercises conducted by skilled facilitators often propelled incredible personal change.

And so it was that the Universe conspired to bring Christina and me closer in a cleverly circuitous fashion. My husband, who was at the time struggling with undiagnosed bipolar disorder—and I was struggling with *him* —eventually ended up attending the first in the series, called the Pursuit of Excellence. Another business owner had recently attended the class, and aware of my husband's challenges, told him to go, suggesting the class would help him. So, my husband and the father of my two sons attended. And he changed. He fucking changed! His behavior was noticeably different, at least short-term. Many of my complaints had no more reason for existence. You'd think I'd be happy about that, but no, I was pissed off. How come, after all my helpful suggestions, he responded to a goddamn course? Huh? I mean, shit. Why *that* and not me? Of course, I was pretty much pissed off about most things back then. Fear will do that.

Part of the process during the initial five-day Pursuit program was breaking up the thirty to forty participants into small groups of four or five people, a standard group dynamic practice. You really got to know your small group members. It's hard to hide for five days with only five people. Each group had a small team leader, a volunteer who acted as a mini facilitator. There were controls in place to ensure the quality and integrity of those volunteers. Christina was one of them, and a couple of times a year would take time out from her busy schedule to be on a Pursuit team so she could donate her time, energy, and calm wisdom helping the members of her small group achieve their desired results. She was awesome at it.

But back to me.

My husband returned from his Pursuit attendance in July of 1989, and began acting differently: calmer, less angry, less sad. Then, he asked me to go with him to an information evening, called an Introductory Session, a scheduled follow-up ten days after he completed the Pursuit. That made me suspicious; I knew it was probably geared toward getting me to take the class myself. Ha! But I went, because a good wife would, don't you know, but I sure wasn't going to take the classes. No way. He was the one who needed help, not me. I was fine, thank you. *Fine*, I said!

But the speaker—the top program leader from Seattle for Context at the time, it turned out, who had been flown out east to lead my husband's program—was so clear, calm, and confident, so real and warm, that I begrudgingly began to believe that perhaps there might be something to be had for myself. But sign up? Give it a chance? Nope. Way too much pride. Way too much fear.

Once his presentation ended, I turned to exit the large hotel meeting room where dozens of recent graduates milled about with smiles I both envied and doubted. My husband was chatting with some of these happy people. Lots of people stood at the sign-up table handing over their credit cards. Not me. I headed out the double-wide doors toward the garishly carpeted hallway beyond.

And there stood Christina, leaning against one of the doors in a tailored white dress. Heels. Crisp, clean, confident. Just standing there, leaning, smiling, relaxed as could be.

"Christina! What are *you* doing here?" I asked with

surprise, and before she could answer added, "You thinking of taking this thing?"

"I already have, Cindy. Out in Seattle. Three years ago. I've told you that before." It was a gentle reminder, not chastisement.

"Seriously? When? I don't remember."

"A couple of times. Over lunch." She straightened up, away from the wall.

"Oh."

Christina smiled, gently. "You weren't ready to hear it."

She was probably right. "Okay, but why are you here tonight then?"

"I was on the team. I was a group leader. It's part of the deal, to be here on Completion Evening."

"Oh. Got it."

"Actually, I was Rob's team leader."

"What? You're kidding me!" I was speechless for a moment.

Holy smokes! Wait a minute. *Wha-a-t?* This woman I so admired had been part of affecting my husband's behavioral changes. She had already taken the class. Could this be a part of why she shone so brightly? It took a second for the information to sink in. She had not even hinted at this connection to my husband, though we had talked several times since he had completed the course. She knew all about my struggles with him. Yet, she had kept her experience with him in complete confidence.

I found my voice. And I remember this moment in technicolor and surround sound vividness.

"Tell me the truth," I said. I stood stock still and looked into her eyes. "Was it worth it, taking the classes?" I needed to know.

Returning my gaze, unblinking, she replied, "Best investment I ever made."

And that was it. Without another word, I whirled to my left, reentered the room, marched myself to the sign-up table, and handed over a credit card. Two weeks later, I attended the class. It changed my life, quite literally, and perhaps, even saved it, at least figuratively. That was 1989, and I dove in head-first. By 1990 I was conducting the back-end program called the Advancement of Excellence, and apparently, was a natural at it, a born facilitator. All I knew was that I loved it, that I came alive in a way I had never before experienced. It seems that's a common experience when one collides with their calling.

By 1994 I had been bumped up to leading the Pursuit, the front-end program, the most difficult to conduct, and the most glorified if you could cut it. (That was also the year my husband divorced me. It was a hard year.) An interesting aspect of my preparation was that the same top program leader who had led my husband's Pursuit ended up training me. With endless patience he helped me shed a few masks and grow from the inside out. At the time, there were only twelve of us who had developed the trust-building skills required to engage with a room full of participants for that front-end program. The one where participants, like me, often engage in defensive, deflective discourse. I was one of those difficult participants in my original class. This is why I've had a soft spot for them since and is perhaps one reason for my continued success in reaching even the stubbornest of clients; I know how scared they are inside. Like I was.

Eventually, I also began leading the middle class, a five-day retreat and a very different experience from the front and back end courses of the three-part series. After my first year leading the Wall, as it was called, I became the top Wall Leader, quite a feather in my cap at the time. And probably one of the biggest reasons for *that* was Christina.

I was scared shitless to conduct my first Wall program, despite my success leading the other two programs. I called Christina, who had moved back to Idaho, and asked if she'd be on my first team. She didn't think twice. "Of course," was all she said. She took time out of her life, flew herself out east, and donated her strength to me during that first, tentative—and emotional—experience. Her reassuring presence and listening ear helped me hang on to some ragged semblance of confidence and enabled me to lead what, in hindsight, I can now assess as a remarkable class, both raw and real. She was my needed mirror for that program as I waved the conductor's wand. She was the sheet music upon whose accuracy and truth I could depend—and have ever since.

We had attended several courses together since my initial participation at the Pursuit, but it was after that first Wall experience that our friendship took on a mutually understood permanence—an irrevocability. Something that which cannot be broken, no matter what.

Over the subsequent years, though separated by physical distance, through divorce and cancer and career changes and all manner of relationship issues, we listened to and supported and guided each other. Before the days of email, we used to write long, hand-written letters, pages and pages of loose-leaf paper filled with words. Letters that read as though we were sitting side by side, the shorthand of best buddies speaking in ink. These letters were treasured when they arrived, and we created a ritual: save the received letter for a quiet evening, pour a glass of wine, and devour the letter twice with utter glee. Of course, the wine might have helped that.

Ah, the indelibility of the written word! Our letters were a reflection of permanence, of our friendship. They were something to hold on to. Words. Connective tissue. Fragments of memories frozen in ink.

I wish I had saved those letters.

5

BEND AND TWIST, NO BUENO

C hristina stands in front of her massive refrigerator, both sides of the double-doored appliance swung wide open to reveal its potential lunch provisions. She surveys the shelves, takes a mental inventory, closes the doors, and then turns at the waist as she bends over to check the freezer compartment below. Her hand rests on the top of the large drawer handle, about to pull it open. She stops suddenly and her face contorts.

"What?" I ask.

She sucks some breath through her teeth the way you do when you stub your toe, waits a beat, then answers.

"Pain." She straightens up slowly and her right hand creeps from the freezer handle to her lower back. This is the first time I've witnessed pain stop her in mid-motion.

"Bend and twist," she finally says, *"este es no bueno."* She turns to face me where I sit at the kitchen counter watching her. I love to watch her cook; she takes so much joy in it and joy in sharing it. I take joy in sharing in her sharing. It's the least I can do.

"I can bend," she says. "And I can twist. Just not at the same time." She chuckles. "Bend *and* twist, *no bueno.*

Remind me when I forget. You've got to do the bending and twisting for me. Can you grab the fish from the freezer?"

She turns to pull the cutting board from its nearby slot and begins chopping some veggies for the salad — fresh cucumbers and tomatoes and scallions straight from the *tienda* that morning — her large, strong hands operating the knife with practiced precision. I retrieve the fish from the freezer drawer, noticing as I do so that I, too, must bend and twist to pull it free from its frozen neighbors. And I notice that when I do, I make the movement unconsciously. Without even thinking about how my body *should* move, it just moves. I take those automatic functions for granted. Things like bending and twisting and breathing and pooping — we take them for granted until we can't do them anymore.

I remember when I had to relearn how to walk after shattering my left knee six years ago. When I tried to take my very first tentative step after eight weeks in a steel enforced leg brace, I could not remember how I used to walk. And that frightened me. My brain had become entrained to a new way of walking, straight-legged, and I had to consciously think about how to move my leg and knee and ankle in unison all over again. It was hard and humbling. And now Christina needs to do the same thing, relearn how to move, in the face of increasing pain. How will she be able to cook or garden or paint without a bend and twist move in her repertoire?

"There are two fronts to this battle," she explains as she chops. "There's the cancer itself and how to manage it, and then there's the pain, and managing that." She stops chopping, puts the knife down and wipes her hands off on the sides of her apron with short, swift slapping motions. Then she uses them to count off her war plans to me. She raises her right index finger.

"First, for the cancer. Food: no sugar. Only fresh food. And I eat two Moringa seeds each morning. They are a natural anti-cancer agent. You should eat some, too, while you're here," she says with a raised brow, ever the big sister. "I've got a bag in my bedroom. Toto picks 'em for me. Fortunately, I've got a tree on the property." She smiles, shrugs her shoulders, and spreads her arms wide. "Who knew?"

She raises another finger, "Second, I drink guanabana tea."

"What? What's that?"

"Anti-inflammatory. Cancer feeds on inflammation." She turns toward the fish and flicks on the stove top before continuing.

"Say it again."

"What? Say what?"

"The name of the plant."

"Oh. Guanabana."

I try repeating what I think I heard her say but mangle it. Christina laughs. "You sound like me when I first heard about it. Think of the Muppets. Remember that song, Manamana?" She starts singing and I join in. "Just like that," she says, "just change the first 'm' to a 'g' and you've got it. All these years and I hadn't even heard about it, but all the natives know. It's a healing plant. Indigenous. And guess what? There's one in my garden! Toto says Chapa planted it years ago."

She turns her attention back to the stove and pulls a small frying pan over the gas flame. Charcoal-black from years of use, it's a cast iron relic from her mother, one of her go-to things. She pours a bit of olive oil into it before continuing.

"So, you take the leaves of the guanabana plant—maybe four or five of 'em—and boil them in a pot of water." She shrugs her shoulders a little. "The active ingredients, whatever they are, are leeched into the water. Then you cool it overnight. And drink it. I add a little lemon and honey. It's quite good. I've got some in the fridge. Help yourself." She lifts the fresh fish filet, a gift from Leo, who had caught and skinned and chopped it up into serving sizes and delivered it to her the day before, and places it in the now hot oil. The fish starts to sizzle immediately in her favorite frying pan.

"Oh," she says with delight, clapping her hands together at her waist. "There is *nothing* like cooking with gas." She turns to me and laughs out loud, pleased at her own double entendre. The last couple of days have been good ones, filled with gratitude and emptied of pain. She looks back to the stove in front of her and stands there a moment, watching the fish fry. Christina loves her gas stove and sturdy pans like I love my laptop and callig-raphy pens; they're our tools, a medium for our creative expressions. To the casual observer, it might look like she's cooking fish, but I know better. She's admiring life right now, and her life in particular, the life she's built. *That's* what she's doing. Admiring. She's giving thanks, silently, the transparency of her gaze playing pictures in her mind like a silent movie. She's thinking about the effort it took to get that sucker up the side of a mountain and how well worth the effort it has proven to be. I sit and watch her from the tall chair on the opposite side of the kitchen counter, three feet away from her. It is one of my favorite things to do, sit and watch her cook.

"Okay," she says. Christina does that, says okay when switching gears, topic or tone. She raises her left hand and turns back to me. And she's back to the raised fingers, only on the other hand now. "Pain management." One finger up. "For that the most important thing is rest.

I cannot overdo it. I must manage my energy, which helps manage the pain. So, that means we might make plans for a certain day and then that day arrives, and my body says, 'Yeah, no.'"

I interrupt her. "I'm good with that."

She smiles. "I know. That's why you're here." What she means is that she no longer has time for anyone who *doesn't* understand that. And then she picks up where she left off. She raises the second finger of her left hand. "CBD oil. Really great for pain relief at certain levels. It takes away pain and leaves room for the life-force energy to return."

"I really want to avoid pills as long as possible," she continues. "I've had to use them a couple of times, but they make me whacky. And constipated. It got bad in last month. But the edibles really help, too. Nate gets them for me. People bring them. Lizzi brought me some of her brownies." Her right hand waves away any concerns about supply. "There's some in the freezer. Help yourself."

"What kind of dosage?" I enquire. I'm a chicken when it comes to shit you swallow. I'm a smoker; I'm good with one toke, most of the time. I'm still a cheap date, whether merlot or marijuana.

"Ten milligrams per gummy. The brownies are about that, too, I think. One is all I need. It's more about my appetite and sleeping. It helps me sleep." She takes the pan from the stove with her right hand and turns off the flame with her left. All her movements are practiced and smooth and watching her make them brings a smile to my face. But the effortlessness of her practiced perfection, observing it, absorbing it, simultaneously makes me sad somewhere deep down inside. It's a physical ache.

Christina has piled a salad on two plates. As was always our dance, I have set the small table that overlooks the northern vista off the top floor of Casa la Ventana. She places a piece of fish on top of the salads and walks the plates to the table.

"You want some wine?" she asks, and then answers her own question, turning on her heel and marching straight back to the kitchen area. "Doesn't matter. *I* do." She chuckles loudly. "Hell, I'm dying! I can drink wine any damn time I want!"

"Grab two glasses." We both laugh.

Christina returns with a bottle of chilled white wine and two glasses. She takes her seat, pours us each some wine, and lifts her glass.

"A toast," she declares. "Here's to a wonderful visit, a wonderful friendship, and a wonderful life." Silence. She's looking into my eyes, meaningfully. "We are fortunate, we two."

"Yes," I confirm. "We are."

We clink glasses. "Let's eat," she says.

Salads are a mainstay in my home. I eat them as a meal several times a week. This particular salad, on this particular day, tastes particularly delicious. And I feel particularly fortunate because I can bend and twist. That's no small thing. There was once a time when I couldn't.

6

A BUOY IN BOCA

Long ago and far away, I nearly died. I was a few months shy of turning four years old. It's my earliest conscious memory. Momentarily unattended, I slipped down the side of a large rock and slid into the water of the mighty St. Lawrence River. This was before I could swim. (I wasn't wearing a life jacket, but remember, back then we didn't do seatbelts, either.) I remember slowly sliding down the side of the slick rock and sinking below the surface. I remember opening my eyes beneath the water and looking upwards and seeing sunlight shimmering through the water's surface. I remember yelling "Help!" I remember seeing bubbles float upwards out of my mouth. And then I blacked out and sank five feet to the bottom of the river.

Fortunately, my father noticed my absence, glimpsed my body off the rock from which I had slipped, jumped in, and hauled me out of the water and onto the shore. Also fortunate: he happened to be a national-level competitive swimmer, an Eagle Scout, and a life guard. He performed CPR and I survived. With minimal brain damage, it appears. I was very fortunate.

I was also fortunate for another reason, but one which I lacked the vocabulary or capacity to articulate for almost forty years. I had a near-death experience during those few minutes under water. I went *somewhere*, somewhere *else*. It was someplace gentle, and it was peaceful. I met, for lack of a better term, a group of *beings* and recognized them as safe, familiar—familial, in fact, my *true* family. I experienced unconditional acceptance and undiluted love. It was powerful and inviting. I wanted to stay there with them. They communicated, "Not now," but left me with a message. "Do not confuse your current humanity with whom you really are." I'm still digesting that. I have believed I have guardian angels ever since.

Not quite fifty years later, I almost died again. This time from gas, not water.

It was March of 2005. I went to bed one snowy evening, fell asleep, and woke four days later. Carbon monoxide had leaked from the faulty furnace in my home. I was rescued about an hour from death, the nurse said. I was lucky to be alive, she said. But it certainly didn't feel that way at the time. It was like getting hit by a tsunami and it took years to right the capsized ship of my life.

Let me tell you, CO poisoning is a bitch with a whip. It's demanding, invisible, and destructive. CO molecules are four times stronger than oxygen molecules, like big bullies who muscle the oxygen out of your bloodstream, slowly destroying all your vital organs. Time of death depends on how high the level and how long the exposure. I was exposed to lower levels for a longer time. The level of CO in the average bloodstream is normally under ten PPM. When rescued, mine was almost 1700 PPM. And though I looked the same, I wasn't. I was literally broken inside, quite out of my mind, and unable to make decisions. I could barely walk for a while and it took years to recover.

Later, I discovered that as I lay there unconscious, this silent stalker was also slowing strangling my hippocampus, the part of the brain responsible for the formation of new memories. As well, the myelin sheaths of nerve endings had been eaten away, so external sensory stimulation became unbearable. I could not handle loud, crowded places. I still don't like them much. I also became susceptible to anxiety attacks. Other effects included headaches, personality and behavioural changes, impaired vision, and loss of muscle control and balance. But the thing that bothered me the most was how it affected my speech for a while. I could talk, but not smoothly or easily, and could not, for a couple of years, pronounce any word with more than three syllables. It was excruciating.

Once I'd recovered enough to know I would survive, Christina swooped in, in 2008, and whisked me away to Casa la Ventana. She'd just completed it. I saw the stone master place the final few stones to the decorative design outside her front portico. It was the first chance I had for complete rest, and an opportunity to take stock of a future that looked very different from the one I had planned. By the end of the trip, I had made the decision to return the next winter. Christina helped me rent a little place next door. It came with a barely-there bed, one chair, no lamps, no towels, no fry pan, no cutlery or dishes, and one old, dented two-quart pot. *Muy rustica.*

My new winter home sat on top of her neighbor's home, the Cruz's, a large Spanish-speaking family who didn't speak English. I didn't speak Spanish. My struggles with pronunciation were suddenly overlooked. I wasn't the first gringo to wander south and mangle their mother tongue. Fortunately, my charade skills were awesome.

The Cruz's have a large, extended family: brothers, sisters, and cousins everywhere. Their home hosts lots of children, activity, and *musica*, at all hours of the day and night. They have lots of roosters, cats, and dogs, as well. Once, after a series of sleepless nights, I complained to Christina about the endless noise. She smiled and shrugged her shoulders. "It's just life happening. It all 'comes with.'"

There was a lot that 'came with' life in Boca, lessons offered up in the most interesting of forms over the eight seasons I spent atop the Cruz household. One was my roommate, George. George was a two-foot-long reptile — not an iguana, mind you, which are everywhere and fairly placid, but a cousin. He was an ugly, territorial, aggressive, backwoods cousin called a garrobo. He decided to take refuge from the sun one day and crawled into *mi casa* through an air hole at the top of the wall where it met the roof.

The first time I noticed him — my attention being drawn by the insistent scratching sounds his two-inch talons made on the brick walls *of my bedroom* — I was justifiably alarmed and concerned. I thought I had communicated both the urgency and validity of my concerns most effectively by screeching at him, jumping up and down, clapping my hands, and finally resorting to poking him with a long stick.

Apparently, something got lost in translation. He crawled further into the cranny under the roof, and never left.

For seven years, George greeted me each winter when I arrived. Eventually, he brought home a new friend—I dubbed her Georgina—with whom he produced several generations of progeny. After fruitless attempts to thwart their homesteading, we came to a mutual understanding of sorts. A détente. A kind of respectful tolerance. They stayed on their beam, away from my bed. I stayed in my bed, away from their beam.

From George I learned acceptance. Sometimes you gotta agree to disagree—and make peace with those who share your space.

Then there was Mattie, my landlord's dog. Mattie 'came with' Boca too. Mattie, and all her ticks and fleas. Everyone in town knew Mattie; she was famous for surviving several litters of pups. She was eight years old when I met her. She would come upstairs every day and nap on my balcony—which she considered hers—with utter disdain for me unless I had food to offer. It took me five years of consistent, intentional effort to earn her affection and trust. It took waves of compassion wearing down rocks of indifference every year, but I did it. She eventually treated me as a member of her family. Mattie taught me that love, just like water, always wins in the end. She died last year, a year after her dear mistress, and my landlady, Silvia, Toto's mom, died. I miss them both.

Another thing that 'came with' life in Boca was the water. It's everywhere. The town is built on, supported by, and a slave to the sea and her moods. The mountain-fed river shapes the fisherman's entrance to the ocean each year after rainy season. The rushing river rises ten feet and moves the lagoon sand all over the place. The entrance is different every year.

But, though water was everywhere, all *around* me, every day, it was rarely available *to* me, in*side mi casa, any* day. Some days, I got running water, some days not.

Some days I got a bit of hot water, but mostly not. And never both hot *and* cold running water at the same time. At least, not in my shower. I tried to have it repaired. I always got the same answer from local plumbers and my landlord. *"No se!"* So, I learned how to bath myself with just two quarts of water warmed in the sun, in a dented old pot, at the end of each day. Boca taught me to value the small things, to notice and appreciate the things I took for granted, like water, and simply waking up in the morning.

It was a simple lifestyle, with small pleasures and a respect for nature, yet fraught with the same human foibles and family dramas found anywhere. Being in Boca helped me rebuild a physical, emotional, and spiritual foundation. And I forged a deeper belief system, one that enabled me to find firmer footing on a shore I didn't even know I was seeking, the one on which Christina had landed after her brush with death. A life of simplicity and connection.

Over those years, I gradually healed more completely, or at least as much as I was going to. I only experience a couple of long-term effects, like short-term memory and balance issues, both of which emerge when I'm tired, so I'm more careful about getting enough rest and eating well. Christina showed me how, having had to manage them herself during her first battle with cancer. She did not simply *help* me recover, she was a critical part of it, carting me to the hospital when I become ill with a severe ear infection. Or that time I got food poisoning from bad shrimp. I had to get a shot in my ass for that. Christina reassured me that the locals treated most things that way, with a shot in the ass.

At that time in my life, adrift in a turbulent sea, Christina provided a buoy to which I could cling. If there is such a thing as reincarnation, we must have known each other before, must have loved each other before, because the trust factor is too deep for it to be a first-time thing. Believing that comforts me.

My second dance with death brought me to Boca. Christina's third brings me back.

7

SMALL DELIGHTS

It is quieter and far less busy in Boca during May. There are fewer tourists stopping by and no B&B guests; they've headed north back to their homes. And it's hotter, with sauna type humidity, than during my previous traditional winter stays. Rainy season approaches. Even sitting in the shade, quiet and still, elicits sweat. We're like dripping sponges. Christina and I head to her pool every day after lunch to avoid the noon-time temperatures and sizzling sun.

"Gawd, it's hot!" I say.

"Yes, it usually is this time of year," Christina says.

"Seriously. How do you manage?"

"This pool. It's a lifesaver." She shoots me a grin. "Well, so far. It won't be in a few months." She's silent a second. Her eyes sweep around the pool area and its surrounding gardens. "I do so love it. It turned out well. Even better than I hoped, in some ways."

She nods toward the wall Chapa built, filled with its own small stone treasures—starbursts and spiral designs —back when Chapa was her garden guy. Christina had someone for everything. It was a running joke. Need something? Ask Christina. If something needed to be repaired or replaced, she knew a guy: a metal man, a massage man, a window guy, a plant lady, a taco guy, a fish man, a cheese man, a bread lady. Chapa was her garden guy back when Casa la Ventana was first built. She had given him free reign to build the large garden retainer wall. The result had exceeded her expectations.

"I don't know how much longer I'll be able to make it down here." Her voice is smaller. She gives her head a small shake, raises her eyes skyward, and says, "But I'm here today! With you." She turns to me and smiles. "Life is good."

I smile in return. "Yes, it is. And it's especially good right now." Especially good because she's still alive, and still the same, on the outside, at least. How will it be when she's not? How will she look and sound then? How will I respond to her?

I am suddenly frightened of the future, of these questions, but mostly by her vivid nearness, the companionable closeness a visceral reminder of its impending disappearance.

One day Christina finds a small piece of plastic on the poolside patio. About the size of a quarter, it appears to be some sort of Mickey Mouse hand that must have broken off its host's body some time ago. Its weathered, white-gloved fingers are curled into a thumbs up position, as though it had been hitchhiking before its untimely demise. Christina picks it up, turns it over in her hands, and then looks around the pool. I sit in a sling-back lounge chair watching her. I want to imprint details. I want to memorize her movements through assiduous study. I want to imprint her, alive, on the screen saver of my brain. The sun sits high in the sky behind us in the midmorning light, casting Christina's shadow on the concrete patio. It outlines her body in perfect black anonymity. Void of wrinkles or tumors, it seems to me to be the shape of her soul, the outline of a life reflected on the cement.

Her eyes wander around the pool area, slowly, deliberately, and then she moves down the steps and into the pool. Her movements are relaxed, languid. She pushes through the chest-high water, gliding slowly toward the opposite side of the pool where the top of the immense retaining wall emerges from below. This wall runs along the entire width of the property along its northern edge, opposite Chapa's decorative garden wall. It's a huge, heavy thing, made of large pinkish rocks, limestone in nature, full of the kind of crevasses ants are particularly fond of, constructed and held in place with grey cement. While we continue to chat, me watching her more than talking, she stops at the edge, leans forward, and fingers a shallow indentation in the massive wall that sits only one foot away from the pool's edge. Reaching out, she carefully wedges Mickey or Minnie's dismembered hand into the walls' small handhold.

"There," she says, then chuckles. "For *los niños* to find the next time they come to swim."

I feel chagrined watching her. I would have tossed the broken fragment in the trash without a thought. Christina finds value in a silly, little broken piece of plastic. She takes things and transforms them into tiny treasures, her delight magnified through the discovery by others.

Note to self: *I must take recycling more seriously.*

We lounge and chat. She's in the water, wandering around the perimeter of the pool. She's examining its condition. Evaluating. I'm content to observe and quite used to this process of hers. Her eyes are always on the lookout for ways to beautify. There is always room for refinement in Christina's world. She reaches out and touches the side of the pool where the patio and pool wall meet. Two horizontal borders, comprised of a series of two-inch square tiles, line the top of the entire pool right beneath the top edge. The lower stripe is a two-inch-wide border comprised of patterned tiles. Above it sits another two-inch border of cerulean blue tiles. The water level sits smack dab in the middle of this top blue stripe.

"I should have put it below the waterline—it shows the salt. I should have flipped these two rows." She's reviewing decisions, looking backwards, exploring her own nooks and crannies; she's run out of time to correct them. I see only the finished product and its elegance. She sees all the things she's learned, what she'd do differently next time. If reincarnation is real, I think we probably do the same thing, review the project, figure out what we'd do differently next time, look for ways to improve. The question becomes, improve for what reason, toward what end? Based on results, the human species, it can be argued, has rather fucked up the planet. I mean, really, why are we here? We better figure it out before there's nothing left to even bother trying to fix.

The metal gate swings open. "Leo!" I smile broadly and get up from my chair to greet him. This is the first time we've seen each other in a couple of years. We embrace.

"I heard you were here." Leo chuckles over my shoulder at Christina. "And how is the queen today?" He delivers it more as a statement than a question. Christina gives him a small dismissive wave. They see each other all the time and she recognizes his impish tone. Leo likes to poke the bear.

"It's fuckin' hot." Leo is also a master of the obvious. "I came to cool off." He's wearing his bathing suit and a well-worn, floral T-shirt, a sleeveless one. He looks like a fashionista's worst generalization of a tacky tourist. He pulls the effrontery over his head in one swift motion, revealing a barrel chest and burgeoning belly. Leo's not fat by any means—he hardly appears overweight with a shirt on—but he rubs his mid-section with flat palms and smiles as he says, "Winter weight. I'm working on taking off a few pounds. I gotta make room for more tequila." He laughs. Leo likes to laugh. Leo likes his tequila, too, but is very disciplined about it. Watching him and Christina float in the pool, it occurs to me that just as I've never seen Christina run, I've never seen Leo drunk.

Leo will turn seventy this year. You'd never know it. If you saw him walking down the street, you'd swear he was in his mid-fifties. His fine, wavy hair is still brown and his face fairly line-free. His hip bothers him some, but overall, Leo is unusually healthy. He says it's clean living. It could be, but I think genes have something to do with it. That and Leo's strictly enforced no-stress rule. He doesn't do drama, won't tolerate fools—according to him there are a lot of folks who fall into the fool category —and lives by certain rules, one of which is you need to mind your own damn business unless asked for input. And even then, best not to give it, it'll only get you into trouble. If you want to see what separating from stress looks like, Leo is the poster child for a successful divorce.

He lives behind a steel door in a second story open-air apartment on the south side of the river where it meets the ocean, maybe a football field away from Christina. He snagged it over a decade ago. He's got a twenty-year lease at about $200 a month. Leo can sit at his one table in the kitchen/living area and watch the world wander by on the beach or the *malecon* in complete anonymity. He can see *them*, but no one can see *him* seeing them, which is exactly the way Leo likes it, safe behind a steel door, able to see what's out there without being required to interact with it. Call it a survivor's thing. After serving in the Vietnam war, Leo came home, gritted his teeth, and worked his way to enough financial freedom that he could escape pressure and find peace. Trauma leaves its mark on a person, in one way or another, and pain sears its brand on your heart. For Leo, the salve for both have been provided by this tiny town, his few fierce friendships, and his devotion to Christina.

"So how long you here for?"

"Two weeks. Our girl time." I smile at him. "But you're allowed, Leo. You're one of the girls."

He chuckles. "Just what I've always wanted, to be one of the girls."

Christina joins us at the side of the pool where the wide, well-placed steps allow for many butts to find comfortable parking spots in the warm water. She took that into consideration when she designed it, wanting a way for many people to have comfortable access to a small pool. She wears a bikini and her radiation burns show above her left breast like visible war wounds. And while she won that battle fifteen years ago, and the one that followed, this one, well, she has not the storehouse to supply a winter battle. A prolonged siege is beyond her capacity at this stage. So, she has planted the white flag outside her door and surrendered to cancer's larger army.

There is no shame in surrender, though the word carries the stigma of such. Perhaps surrender doesn't mean you're giving *up*, but rather giving *in*, letting go. Going *with* the tide instead of struggling against it. The question becomes when to hang that flag, when and how to realize you're fighting a tide in your life.

Questions. Sometimes, I am exhausted by my questions. But I find the fact that I even choose to ask them —regardless of my ability to formulate cogent answers—

slightly reassuring, at some level. As though I'm on the right road but driving toward an unknown destination without a map. You can use a lot of gas that way. And you can end up driving in circles, but at least you're still moving, which can fool you into thinking you're making headway. This is reassuring to those of us who still mistake motion for meaning and persistence for purpose.

8

BIG DECISIONS

"Don's not well." Christina sat at the wheel of her trusty, dusty, monster SUV.

We were on our way home from one of our Costco trips, laden with supplies. This was maybe five or six years ago, before the second re-emergence of her breast cancer. At this point in her life all was well. She was years out from her original cancer, her new home was complete, and she had a regular stream of B&B guests whose stays covered the costs of running Casa la Ventana. She was busy, healthy, and happy. But her husband wasn't. She had a plan every day, something to do, to create, and a purpose that propelled her. Her husband didn't.

"What do you mean?" I had asked her.

"There's something wrong." She paused. "I think it might be dementia. Early stage. He keeps forgetting things." As was her way, Christina got right to the point. When she wanted to discuss a concern that was on her mind, this was how she'd start. No dancing around a subject, she'd dive right in.

"I just found out he forgot to pay his Visa bill again.

And he's supposed to transfer money to the *Casa* account but forgets. I explain why and where the money goes, every month, and every month it's the same questions all over again." Christina chewed her bottom lip. "I'm not sure what to do about it. It's speeding up my longer-term decisions."

"Man. Sorry. That stinks." The windows were open, the car's speed diffusing the heat, the breeze soothing our skin. We drove in silence for a bit. My mind played out the implications. "You thinking power of attorney?"

"Eventually, yeah. But it's getting from here to there." She turned to look at me. "I've done the research. It's not a pretty path."

"And the VA? He's got good coverage, right?" Don had served in Vietnam in the sixties and received superior U.S. veteran benefits.

"Only if he actually seeks medical assistance. He needs to acknowledge it first, and he won't. He thinks it's age." She turned and gave me a pointed glance. "It's not." Her eyes returned to the road. "And . . . he gets angry . . ." She paused before continuing. "Sometimes, frankly, he frightens me."

Not long afterwards, they moved to separate bedrooms, not out of any ill will or rancor, but rather a result of divergent rising and retiring routines. It was the first step towards separation. Over the intervening years, she got him to the VA hospital back in the States and ultimately was able to get power of attorney and a handle on their finances. But it was a painstaking, incrementally slow process with progress measured in inches.

After her most recent diagnosis, she was done. She asked Don to leave Casa la Ventana just weeks before I arrived for our special two-week visit. Actually, it was more like she told him he had to go. That she's dying and she can't care for him anymore. He doesn't understand.

Now, in the mid-stages of dementia, he is able to walk
and talk, and from a distance appears to be fine, normal,
but his balance, memory, and cogent thinking ability has
declined dramatically over the past five years.

Don and Christina met after she moved away from Baltimore. She had decided that when her contract for the
homebuilder ended, she wanted to travel to Central and
South America. In preparation, Christina labeled everything in her home in Spanish. There were three-by-five-
inch cards taped everywhere, to everything: the T.V., the
stove, the door, the window, the food in the cupboards.
Those things were stuck there for almost a year! Then,
looking to practice her growing vocabulary, she opened
her home to a Spanish-speaking exchange student for the
summer. Before she moved, Christina could speak the
language well enough to get by.

What she couldn't do, however, was set out on a
journey to uncertain parts of the world alone. She
needed a traveling companion, a male one. She put out
the word, and before long, a friend of a friend and she
had connected and started to formulate a plan of action
and a timeline for departure. This was to be a minimum
of six months on the road. Christina was a consummate
camper. And the new friend also had a friend, named
Don, who ended up tagging along at the last minute.
Both guys were taller than she, so she left feeling
secure, but a couple of weeks into the trip the first guy,
with whom she'd grown comfortable and close, had a
family emergency and had to return home. This left
Christina and Don to make a decision. They could
either continue or abort the trip. They decided to carry
on. At some point they must have also grown comfort-

able and close, too, because a couple of years later they married.

A well-meaning and nice enough guy, Don lacked the ambition and initiative Christina harbored and the work ethic she held dear. He pooh-poohed her dedication to self-awareness and self-improvement. He denigrated homosexuals, something she found intolerable. I had heard a lot of Don stories over the years, enough to know that the marriage had been dormant for a decade at least. Eventually, contempt crept in.

Now, after over five years of doing her very best to assist Don in adjusting to a condition he stubbornly still refuses to acknowledge, let alone accept—nor will he allow her to help him with it—Christina's done. Don is unwilling to accept either his diagnosis, or hers. He understands cancer. He beat prostate cancer over a decade ago, close on the heels of Christina's original breast cancer. He survived, she survived. In his mind, she'll survive again; death doesn't compute. He is angry and sad and confused but doesn't really know why. All he knows is he isn't getting what he wants, which is continued unfettered access to Casa la Ventana without contributing toward its well-being and upkeep, physically or emotionally. Though Christina continued to cook for him, made sure he had clean clothes, and cared for him, this final physical separation had been many years in the making. His presence in the house, at this time of transition for her, was too large a drain on her dwindling energy.

Well over six feet tall, Don used to be lanky but now carries a bit of a potbelly, not an uncommon condition for older men who have a history of heavy beer consumption. He used to be pretty handy, too, but now his fingers are twisted and misshapen by arthritis. His shoulders are hunched. He used to be quite a drinker,

but not so much anymore. Christina put her foot down in
the early years of building up her B&B business. She
couldn't have a tall, drunk husband wandering the
grounds causing the guests to second-guess their destination decision. In her ten-year history of running Casa la
Ventana, she never lost a guest, no matter the problem.
From no water to an errant husband, Christina's forceful
clarity and compassion and competence won people over
quickly, easily, and permanently.

These days, Don is increasingly irritable. He
complains a lot, about almost anything, a symptom of the
illness that's slowly stealing his mind. Christina has not
been harsh or angry or sad with him, but she has been
firm because unlike Don she is *not* confused. She is clear
as a bell. She knows how she wants to die and where she
wants to direct her energy and with whom she wants to
spend her remaining time. Don is not part of that
equation.

He moved only a few weeks before my arrival mid-
May, to a small suite with an ocean view just a kilometer
down the road from Boca. He comes by toward the end
of my first week to pick up some more of his belongings.
He has collected a lot of stuff over the years, Christina
wants his stuff gone. She doesn't care what he does with
it as long as it's out of her space. She's been planning his
move for months, encouraging him to reach out to his
only son from whom he has been estranged for many
years. Christina no longer has room for the space his
physical or emotional stuff consumes and has helped
organize what is his into large plastic containers. Don
finds packing overwhelming. Goodbyes are beyond his
grasp.

I support her decisions, of course, and understand
why she made this one, but I can't help but feel a little
sorry for Don when I see him carrying a large box slowly

down the stairs, his aging, knotted fingers gripping the edges of his remaining memories. He doesn't understand. And there's nothing Christina can do about that except to continue to establish boundaries, clearly and compassionately, and at the same time firmly, too. You have to do that, be firm. Because old folks and young children can have difficulty accepting restrictions or change.

9

NIGHT SWIMMING

They say a high tide lifts all boats in a harbor. Christina's laugh lifts all people within earshot. She laughs easily and often and the sound of it alters the atmosphere of a room. But her walk? Her walk will *slo-o-w* you down.

Christina doesn't walk the way I walk, which is to *get* somewhere, and to get there in an efficient fashion. In other words, strolling is for lovers, not ladies with appointments. I learned to walk quickly as a child, trying to keep up with my father's longer strides. I admit to feeling as though I must always slow my normal pace to accommodate others, even men. From my perspective, Christina *walks* nowhere—she lopes. Some people stroll, some shuffle, some sashay, others stride. Christina lopes. Her body sort of gently undulates up and down when she walks, rather than side-to-side. There's not a lot of hip action, but then, not a lot of hips. She's all legs, all the time. And not a single dot of cellulite to be seen. She's an aberration of nature.

Christina seems always to be in slow motion, never rushed. Even when I know she feels rushed on the inside, her walk never reflects it. She has never moved quickly—her mind, yes, her body, no. I've never seen her run. She has always been deliberate. Now, she lopes toward an uncertain future whose horizon has shortened, deliberate about her undetermined destination. Like a cruise ship, with ports of call void of landing dates, she knows where she's heading, but not when she'll arrive.

Today, Christina parks the car on the cobblestone side street of Puerto Vallarta's *Zona Romantica* and we walk to her current favorite little nail salon. She has made appointments for us to get mani-pedis. We stop three times within two blocks for reasons unknown, reasons previously undeclared. I stand and wait, hovering nearby as she chats with whomever she's inter-acting. It's what I do, hover and wait.

Note to self: I must learn more Spanish than I currently command. A lot more.

Once inside and after some more chirpy Spanish greetings and hugs, we choose a nail color and settle into our side-by-side seats. We are the only customers. There are two ladies tending to us, the owner, Christina's friend, Luisa, and her niece. They scurry around, filling tubs with water. Christina and I begin soaking our feet in warm soapy water while the ladies wheel trays of tools into place. They undertake the task of transforming our hands and hooves from plow horses to thoroughbreds worthy of strutting our stuff, not that there's much stuff left to strut, but what little there might be—like our finger and toenails—we want to wave around with pride and panache.

The three of them chatter away in Spanish. I catch a word here and there, but for the most part check out. I close my eyes and listen to the music playing in the back-ground. It appears to be a station mired in the eighties. Tune after tune, that's the whole playlist. *Take On Me*, by

A-ha. *Wake Me Up Before You Go-Go* from Wham!. Queen, *Crazy Little Thing Called Love*. Michael Jackson, Bette Midler, Kenny Loggins, The Cars, U2, and more. I start singing along, much to the amusement of Christina. She smiles but doesn't join in. Come to think of it, I've never heard her sing. Why is that? *You've not noticed before, that's why. Pay attention.*

Here's what I do notice, though. I know every word to every song that comes on, to the point that when one song ends and another is about to start, the ladies stop their filing or painting and look at me. When I break into song again, they burst out laughing and resume their chattering. It becomes a game, a challenge, like Ken Jennings on Jeopardy. When will she be stumped? My short-term memory may not be what it once was, but my long-term memory works just fine, thank you. By the time we leave, our hands and feet are gorgeous and we're in good moods and quite show-worthy.

Tonight is our last night before my flight home. Tonight, I will fulfill my arrival day promise to take her out for a meal on me. We gussy ourselves up a bit, putting on clothes that flow, adding a little eye shadow and lip gloss, and drive the short distance to one of the top restaurants in the PV area, Le Cliffe, a popular wedding spot which boasts the largest *palapa* roof in Mexico. While the food is delicious and the service excellent, it is the view that draws the patrons. Only one kilometer from Boca, it sits at the top of a cliff (hence the name) and boasts an unobstructed 180-degree view of the Pacific Ocean, for miles and miles, with nothing but blue water and a vast horizon of hope illuminated by a setting sun.

A setting sun.

I'm sitting here, at a small table for two, outside the *palapa* covered main dining room, perched on a narrow ledge atop the cliff with only a few additional tables nearby, watching my friend gaze out over the ocean, her hands folded in her lap, at peace, and I suddenly remember that she's dying, that this is our last experience like this, our last time together where she can still walk and laugh and eat with glee. I know that my next visit will be dramatically different; that her bright light will set as certainly as this day's sun will slip below the horizon of visibility; that her body will wither away and her light with it; that this is my last night with her while she still looks the same. *She still looks the same!* How can I begin to let her go? How do I wrap my brain around the fact that I'll *have* to, because she won't be here in the flesh a year from now? And that I'd damn well better figure out how to let her go while she's still here.

"Breathtaking," I remark, referring to the view. "I'm so glad to be here with you."

She turns her head to me and smiles. "Me, too." After a beat she says, "Did I tell you? Joy's coming down after you. Two weeks from now, for a week."

"One-on-one time? Or is she bringing the posse?"

"Just her this time. I think she might come back with all of them over the summer sometime. Not sure when." And then, wistfully, "I do love them all."

She's referring to her surrogate daughter, Joy, and Joy's best friends. They are spiritual sisters. They moved to Colorado together from DeKalb, Illinois in their early twenties, and for over twenty years have celebrated each other's marriages and mourned each other's losses. They've also helped raise each other's kids—all except Joy, who, by choice, never married.

Now in her forties, I first met Joy when she was ten years old. Her older brother married my younger sister. She arrived at my home in Baltimore with her dad, Jim Wiggins, in late June of 1987, the day before the wedding. She had blonde hair, and a bob haircut which framed her young face in an angelic way. I remember opening my front door and seeing her standing there looking up at me, with a beaming smile, all innocent openness and hopeful anticipation. Her big brother, Joe, whom she adored, was getting married, and she was to be in the wedding! But her mom had just died, and her dad didn't know about weddings, so the poor only daughter of a stand-up comic didn't own a proper pair of shoes. As I recall, she had one pair of sneakers. That was it. I took her shopping. She's been a thread in the fabric of my life's tapestry since.

In 2003 Joy attended my signature five-day program entitled The Trust Program, on which I launched my company in 1998. She was still in her twenties. The follow-up to that class, cleverly named The Joy Class (program titles, obviously, are not my thing), I conducted at Casa la Ventana in the winter of 2009. Joy attended that class and met Christina there, who handled all the logistical details and the cooking for a dozen participants. It was an exemplary program. Joy and Christina bonded big time, so Joy continued to visit Boca every year since—or multiple times a year—staying with me several times over the eight winters I spent there. I love Joy like a little sister; Christina loves her like the daughter she never had.

"Remember when she got that 'love' tattoo?" I refer to one of the many tattoos Joy sports in discreet loca-tions on her petite, yoga-toned body. She had the word love permanently inscribed in elegant cursive on her left ankle one winter while in PV.

"Hurts like a bitch," she told us at the time, while thrusting her ankle onto the tabletop of the beachside restaurant where we sat. Her flesh was swollen and red. "But then, so does love sometimes."

She's right. Love can be painful. But the payoff is so worth the inevitable loss of the flesh. We will all die. Everyone. Love, though, doesn't.

Christina chuckles. Her shoulders rise and fall a couple of times. "That girl!" She gives her head a quick shake. "Always something." Her smile broadcasts love.

"Yeah, relationship drama. Gawd, I hope I'm done with that," I say. "Though, I'm still toying with the idea of getting a tattoo."

"You've been thinking 'bout that for years!"

"I know. Just not sure exactly what I want, or why. I know I want a word, but which one? Love? Trust? I kind of need to know both before heading into a parlor, don't ya think?"

"Too bad you didn't do it that Christmas you came with the boys."

"Yeah, it just got too busy." In 2012 we had had a family gathering over Christmas in Boca. My then-single adult sons—with whom I wanted to share Boca visually after many years of gushing verbal descriptions—along with my youngest sister, Jennifer, and her daughter and husband, Joe, and Joy were all there. Christina did the cooking. It was a wild and wonderful week; a once-in-a-lifetime experience; a bookmark memory. Mucho tequila. Enough said.

"So glad we did that–Christmas." It was wonderful being there with Casa la Ventana all dressed up in her holiday best, twinkling lights and cheerful music broad-casting goodwill over the mountainside. My boys loved their time there; I loved their loving it.

"Me, too," Christina says, turning to look at me. We're both remembering. "You've got good boys."

"Thanks, sweetie. All those years of self-examination . . . finally paid off, huh?"

"Yeah. Years of focus and work in any area usually

does pay off. I mean, just look at my garden. Only ten years of work!" We both laugh, knowing her extensive gardens are a work in progress, and always will be. Like us.

After finishing our meal, we head home and climb the relentless Stair Monster back to Casa la Ventana. The night air is heavy with moisture, and by the time we reach the front door our clothes cling to our skin. We change into our bathing suits and regroup down by the pool. REM's lyrics from *Night Swimming* float through my brain. There is something sensually delicious about swimming in warm water at night. Buoyancy. Freedom. We lounge in the water, chat in idle spurts, but mostly float and stare at the stars, content in silent companionship. I can feel the impending rending of tomorrow's departure beginning in my gut.

I do not want to leave her. I do not want her to leave me. I do not want the memories to dissipate, to fade over time, like an ice sculpture in the sun. I want them dipped in bronze, like a Bronze Star, forged for permanence, a reflection of honorable service.

But I am no sculptor nor member of the military. And I know that, one day, whether I like it or not, whether I'm ready for it or not, there will come a time when she will be physically gone from my life and the lives of all who love her. My choice will be how I choose to greet that new reality. I pray I might accept it as peacefully as Christina.

"Who were your top three lovers?" Christina's non sequitur severs the silence surrounding us and stops me short.

"What? Where'd that come from?"

She pauses and shrugs her shoulders. Looks back up at the stars. "I don't know. It's just a question."

No, it's more than that, I'm just not sure what yet.

"Um. Let me think about it for a second." I'm buying time, not because I don't want to answer, or that I can't, it's because hidden within the question is the reason why she's asked. Christina is reviewing her life and inviting me to come along. My answers don't matter. Hers do.

"Well, I was married to two men for a lot of years so there really aren't all *that* many."

Christina shoots me a hooded sidelong glance. She knows better. "There were enough." She's right, there were. I've forgotten most of them, though, due to age or irrelevance.

I name someone, pause, and return her glance. "How about you? You got a top lover on your list?"

She does. She talks about him. And she smiles. It's why she asked. She wanted to smile and share a part of her journey. Because her days are numbered, and her lovemaking with them. Pain is on the prowl and she is its prey.

But tonight? Tonight, there are stars and warm water and bellies full of food, hearts full of love, and easy, safe companionship. Tonight, there is only friendship and love. Sisters and secrets.

And the knowledge that, at least for right now, this night, she's still alive.

10

THE TIME BETWEEN

The next day, I fly home, hugging her hard and long when I leave, but keeping it light. "I'll be back," I say before heading inside the airport terminal, and then turn and smile and wave. The time for tears would come, but not now. To allow them would be to acknowledge the impending loss and I'm not ready to do that yet. So, I return to my life, with its business and family commitments, and keep grief at arm's length by staying busy.

Within a couple of months, Christina's face and body reflects the beginning of emaciation. Despite her best efforts, weight falls from her frame like peeling paint falls from a fence in a heavy rainstorm. The increased pain causes her to begin to rely on opiates more often, but they play havoc with her bowels, so she tries to keep her opiate use to a minimum. She keeps her spirits up, most days, and people come by to visit or help, and Leo is there as her go-to guy, but I can hear the changes in her voice over the phone, and while she can still make it down to the pool, slowly, I suddenly realize Christina won't last much beyond the new year.

One day, three months after our visit, in early August of 2018, Christina and I were having one of our regular catch-up calls, again on a Sunday. She told me her son and his wife and their children were coming for a visit at the end of the month. This was a big deal; she hadn't had any quality time with her grandsons in several years and looked forward to seeing them in a way a starving person looks forward to food. She was desperate to reconnect with them and Christina wasn't desperate about much, ever.

"Nothing like impending death to repair relationships," she said to me. "Speeds up the timeline."

The family planned to return for two weeks at Christmas. That, too, was a bright spot of light on the distant horizon. Something to look forward to, to keep her eyes and heart trained upon.

But I worried about the way she sighed when she added, as an aside, "I'm pretty sure I have one more Christmas in me." This sent a silent, icy shiver through my body. She would hang on until her son and his family had one last Christmas together—that was her buoy—and then she'd let go. Quickly.

"How long are they staying?" I asked. "How soon after they leave can I arrive?" I had intended to visit her for the entire month of February.

"They'll leave the day after New Year's, I think. Come any time after that." She paused and I was about to say something when she added, "But don't wait too long."

That day, after hanging up the phone, I changed my trip to January. I had to see my big sister one more time in the flesh before her voice and light faded. I had to pay attention. And I wanted to chronicle the experience, capture it, and imprint it in my memory bank for all time. Bronze it.

∼

I packed a tiny bag, because less is better in Boca. I made sure to include the power chord for my laptop, my preferred mechanism for daily data capturing and imprinting, and the way I sort through stuff and try to make sense of it. I decipher life that way.

I made arrangements with my neighbor and good friend, Sally, to tend to my plants. Sally has two cats. I babysit them when she leaves town. But Sally doesn't really do plants in her own place. The cats chew on them or step in them or knock them over. So she stopped by my apartment the night before my flight to see exactly which plants will require watering and where they reside. Sally likes accuracy.

"How often?" she asked when I gave her the door key. I had made a copy for her.

"It depends on how cold it gets and how hard the heat pumps. I'm cutting it way back to seventeen degrees when I leave, so they shouldn't need too much water over three weeks. Maybe once, midway."

"I'll check every week." Sally is diligent and thorough. Caution runs in her blood.

"I'll leave them well watered. Once should do it, maybe ten days after I leave. A thorough soaking. You might want to do the smaller ones over the sink —except for the big boy in the corner. Leave him where he is. One full jug for him is good." I showed her my watering jug.

"Okay." She looked at the key in her hand. "This works, right?"

"Test it," I said. I've learned not to speed through Sally's yellow lights. She tested the key in my front door lock, turned it back and forth a couple of times, and seeing that it worked, she relaxed. There is a plan in place, a structure to support it, and access in order to execute it.

"So sorry about your friend." She knew the reason for my upcoming absence. Sally is the essence of empathy.

"Yeah, well . . . it's okay." She was trying to be nice, but I wasn't sure what to say about the reality of Christina's certain—and too soon—exit. "I mean, it's *not*, but, you know, there's no stopping cancer. I mean, this is it. She's on the way out. I've had a few months to wrap my brain around it. We'll see if my heart gets onboard once I'm down there."

"Yeah." Sally gave me a wry smile. "Good luck with that."

"Thanks, Sal," I said, reaching out to give her a hug goodbye. "I'll need it."

11

HOUSTON, I'VE SCREWED THE POOCH

I've known some pain in my life, both emotional and physical. Haven't we all? But there are degrees, and pain is both subjective and relative. I used to take pride in (what appears to be) my quite high pain threshold, but with hindsight, I wonder if I might have been rather stupidly daring the Universe to test me. Life has a way of doing that, wrecking your plans, smashing your compass, blowing you off course. Like a hurricane. Or, like a mobster with a baseball bat. Life can take you out at the knees.

I went to the cottage during the Independence Day holiday weekend of July 2013, arriving ahead of the hordes scheduled to descend over the long weekend. Since I live closest, I usually get there ahead of the others to make sure the beds are made, towels are available, milk is in the refrigerator, etcetera.

Christina and I had had a chatty catch-up call late that Friday morning, during which I had reiterated my desire for her to visit me, and we had made plans for the following year. She would be my *plus one* for my son's wedding in Baltimore, and we would travel together to the St. Lawrence River where I could finally share my family cottage with her. After we traded our stories for over an hour and said our goodbyes, I cooked up two delicious BLTs on English muffins and ate both. That's unusual for me, two sandwiches, but in hindsight, a rather fortuitous choice that my belly was full before calamity struck.

It had rained hard the night before, and the property was covered in darkened tendrils of earth. The pine needles had been swept away by the mini monsoon. The storm had abated but I could see a darkening sky downriver. Good time to flip the last load of laundry out in the shed, I thought. Get it in the drier. Then bring in another load of wood and stoke the fire. Settle into the comforting silence and solitude of a clean house and a good book before people began arriving.

Ah, plans. You know what they say about making plans. Guess I must have made God laugh.

If I was a professional athlete, the TV announcers would have sucked in their breath and scrunched up their faces. Next, there would have been silence. Respectful mourning. Finally, they would have bemoaned it a career-ending injury.

All I remember is that after schlepping my way out to the shed—which is where the washer and drier stupidly reside—and flipping the laundry load, I turned to exit the shed, took a single step out onto the wood ramp which slants from the doorway to the ground, and slipped on its slick surface. I fell onto my left knee, hard, like a pile driver, and with a force so sudden, so sharp, that my kneecap exploded. Literally. As though God's fixer had taken a tire iron to it. *Had I forgotten to pay some unknown debt?*

After the first operation, twenty-four hours after the fall, the surgeon said that when he opened me up, my kneecap was dust. The refrain from the old Kansas song rolled around my brain and escaped my lips as I sat in the wheelchair waiting for my ride home. I sang my way back to the cottage from the back seat of my son's car. "Dust in my knee, all there is, is dust in my knee." Of course, I was on morphine. My first time. Quite a drug.

At the time of the fall, however, I did not realize that my left knee was now an unhinged appendage from which dangled a useless lower extremity. At the time, given that I was in shock, I can now see that I wasn't thinking clearly at all because here's what I thought was my best option. Since I was approximately fifty yards from the back door of the cottage, I thought my best option was to *hop* there on my still-intact right leg. Uphill and down, over roots and rocks, I thought I could hop my way home. In hindsight, I can now see that this was *not* a good idea. In fact, hopping was a really, really dumb idea. It was the kind of idea about which people say afterward, "I don't know what I was *thinking*."

Hindsight: the ability to see your own ass and assess how awful you look from behind.

I got myself upright, adrenaline coursing through my body with a throbbing energy that narrowed my focus to immediate survival mode. I was alone, on an island, in the middle of a storm, on the Friday afternoon of a holiday weekend. The storm was kicking up again, and the wind with it. There would be no help coming for at least a day. I had no choice but to get to the house. So, I would hop, dammit!

I managed to get up, balancing on my right leg and assuming some sort of crouching position with my arms extended. I thought the position might, somehow, allow me to hop for fifty yards . . . in the rain and wind, over uneven terrain. Think the Karate Kid, and his stance at the end. That's how I looked: arms raised, left leg dangling, eyes focused. This would be the part of the movie where the entire audience knows a very bad, horrible thing is about to happen, but the protagonist, for some ridiculous reason, hasn't a clue. Silly, silly woman.

But I tried anyway. I hopped. Once. The effort and impact of the physical movement caused my newly disabled and quickly swelling blob of what used to be my left knee to wobble wildly. Only my skin held it together. I almost blacked out from the pain. I'd never experienced that before, black pain, the kind that pushes to the edge of consciousness. I dropped to the ground, rolled to my side, and let out a scream that seemed to come from outside myself. I made no conscious choice to scream. It was released, unbidden, in proportion to my pain. It was fucking primal. It was black. I have never screamed like that before, ever, not even during childbirth. The pain sucked me into a vortex of disorientation, as though I'd been consumed by a tornado, left swirling in an enveloping darkness, surrounded by danger. There was nothing to cling to, no walls of support. And no one to help me.

And so began the oddly amusing portion of my awkward crab crawl to the cottage. I've said since that if they ever made a movie of my life, this would be the comic relief portion of the story.

Eventually, after what seemed like an endless hour, I maneuvered my way to the porch, crawled up and onto it, and managed to turn the door handle, and then somehow slither my way inside the house without the door knocking into my useless left leg. Like some large and seriously misshapen snake, I slid my way indoors and for a moment felt invincible. I had achieved the first level on Maslow's scale. Safety. Laying there, immobile on the floor, for one brief second, I had a visceral experience of relief. That's one thing about pain. After an initial adjustment to its current level, any relief is experienced as a sort of victory in the short term, no matter how ineffective it may prove to be in the long term.

Aware that the adrenaline would wear off soon, I hauled myself onto my elbows, pulled myself up on the piano stool, and with my weight on my right leg, my left dangling lifeless, I grabbed my cell phone from the top of the piano. To my delight, once standing upright on my still-intact right leg, I found that just letting my left leg hang—as long as I made no sudden movements—provided a sort of painless experience. I could at least shuffle around. Carefully. Steadied by tabletops and chair backs I slithered my way to a chair and sat down—phone in hand. Moment of truth. Bending over, I began to roll up the left pant leg. When I got to the edge of the knee, I took a deep breath, and looked.

My stomach lurched. I almost threw up right there. It literally looked like Vinnie had taken a tire iron to my knee and smashed it to bits. *Pay up, bitch!* I quickly looked away. I took another deep breath along with two quick photos and texted them to my brother who happens to be an orthopedic surgeon in the States. *I fell on the ramp to the shed*, I wrote. *I think I screwed the pooch*. Within a minute he texted back, confirming that yes, indeed, that pooch had been royally screwed. I needed surgery.

I called emergency for a boat rescue, and an hour later, with an ambulance waiting on the mainland, I was delivered to the nearest hospital in a town of about 20,000 residents. The surgeon on call was notified but had other emergencies and I had to wait until the next day. The adrenaline had worn off and the pain seemed to radiate out from my knee and into every hidden corner of my body. I felt exhausted and scared and lonely and careless to have fallen in the first place. Every cell in my body screamed out for assurances, guarantees to ward off the pain of the present and fear of the future, but there were none to be had.

Pain is like that. It fills the entire container like a gas and creeps into every nook and cranny. Doesn't matter if it's physical or emotional. Pain robs the human organism of its life force, its vitality. Like printing a color document in black and white, pain reduces the landscape of the present to greyscale.

Women talk about the pain of childbirth, and I gave birth, naturally, twice, and yeah, it's painful, but it's a pain with a purpose. There's a baby coming out. Like going to a bummer of a birthday party, at least you get to leave the hospital with a great goody bag, a gorgeous baby bundled in your arms. And there's tooth and ear pain, which I've had, an emergency appendectomy, and a sprained ankle. Things like that. Childhood injuries.

As an adult, however, physical pain, most of the time, seems useless to me. Stupid. A waste of energy. Athletes grow used to it, so they say, but I'm not a big fan of *no pain, no gain*. Screw that. But emotional pain, senseless as it may seem, can become the bedrock for new beginnings. It sends a signal of things *still-to-be-learned* from the soul. Emotional pain—and its spectrum opposite, peace—is the language of our heart, not our mind.

Lying in that hospital bed, alone and broken and in horrible pain, not only did I feel utterly alone and frightened, I felt stupid. The pain screamed at me, "You should have been more careful! How could you let this happen?" Maybe the physical pain wanted a companion and invited intellectual beratement along as its playmate. As though my emotional despair wasn't enough.

But, give me physical pain over emotional pain any day. Broken bones can heal, if the patient follows a doctor's instructions. They will heal according to a somewhat natural progression: at week four this is what one can expect, at eight weeks you can expect to be able to bend *this* or twist *that*. There is a timeline to the relief of the brokenness.

Broken hearts, not so much. Loss of a sense of purpose or direction, loss of friends or family through divorce or death, loss of identity and role, these are the common and communal pain points of the human experience. It is purposeless pain that takes us out at the knees, that cripples us if we let it.

Purposeful pain, though, becomes bearable. It can be carried. Because with a clear purpose, the pain becomes a partner, a reminder of the importance of the purpose behind it. It has a direction and a desired end result and its own propulsion.

I know the direction of my current pain: Christina's death. What's missing is its purpose. I trust it will reveal itself. Or perhaps unearthing some sort of purpose from the landslide of grief is the whole point. Maybe it's not just what propels us forward but is, in fact, the only thing that can.

12

BACK TO BOCA

I touch down at the Puerto Vallarta airport once again on another Friday in January 2019. I have three weeks with Christina this trip—four precious Fridays worth of time—and I remind myself to pay attention to all the days in between. To notice. Everything. I get in line for an airport taxi. Forty-five minutes later, I am deposited next to the Boca bridge where Toto awaits my arrival to carry my bag up to Casa la Ventana, bless him. He holds a sleek new smart phone through which he stays in communication with Christina and Joy.

"Toto! Como estas, mi amigo?"

"Bien, bien. Y tu?"

"Muy bien, gracias." My tone changes. "Y Christina?"

His tone alters, too. His gaze shifts to the ground, and then back to my face. "Oh, no bueno, Cynthia, no Bueno," he says quietly. "Ella esta malo."

"Si." We both shake our heads. With nothing left to say, we head across the bridge and toward the stairway from hell.

I trudge my way up the last section of stairs. Toto has

beaten me by a mile, trotting my suitcase on his shoulder up the endless stairs to Casa la Ventana's grand portico and oversized front door. I've had to stop twice, gasping both times. Too much winter couch lounging.

"You're here!" Joy bounds out the front door and bounces down the top few steps. If she were a cartoon character, she'd be Winnie the Pooh's Tigger. *Woohoo!* "You're here! You're here!" She stops bouncing and wraps me in her arms five steps from the top. "Good to see you, sistah," she says, using the term of endearment some of us have adopted to distinguish between blood sisters and chosen sisters, the latter often more important than the former.

Joy squeezes her arms around my neck. She's a wee thing, just a fraction over five feet tall, and has to reach up as I reach down. Positioned one step above me, we are almost at eye level.

"Oh, it's so good to see you, too!" I reply, squeezing her tight and lifting her off the ground before releasing her.

Her hair is still short and blond. Ten years ago, when she first came to visit Boca and stayed at my place next door to Christina's, both of us had long hair. Independently of each other we both cut it drastically short a few years later and have kept it that way. Her hair is finer and sparser than mine, and it dries in three minutes. Mine, courser and thicker, might take all day to dry when left to its own natural devices in a humid climate. After a shower, all Joy does is squirt some sort of hair product into her palms, rub them together quickly, flip herself over at the waist, and run her hands through the inverted strands as though towel drying her hair. Then she flips herself upwards and checks her reflection in the mirror as she continues to pluck and pull her hair into place. The whole thing takes a minute from start to finish. I've watched her do it. The result is a kind of really cute, spiked, pixie hairstyle that looks great on her. I envy the minimal time investment required by her hair. If I tried the same technique with *my* hair—flipping aside —I'd look like an electrified cartoon character: silly, stupid, and ugly.

I want to see Christina, but Joy tells me she's resting, and that she should be awake shortly.

"How's she doing?" I ask Joy's backside. She's two steps in front of me and I have a bullseye view of her buttocks straining against the woven fabric of her skort. Some would say they're her best feature.

"Better. Christmas freaked me out, though. I really didn't think she'd make it. Had to call Nate and say, 'You better get here quick.' Been eating some, but not enough; she's way too thin. Nate's been cooking for her, which is great." Joy pauses a beat. "But she's ready for them to leave. It's been stressful." Joy gives me a look over her shoulder. "People are getting it, that she's dying. Everybody wants to visit." She gives her head a shake as she bottom-lines it. "She can't handle it."

Joy opens the front door and then veers to her right, into Don's old room. I follow her.

"You're with me for the weekend, until Nate and Karen leave," she says. "Hope you don't mind."

"Hell no," I reply quickly. Nate is Christina's only child, and Karen is his wife. They have been here over the Christmas holidays with their adolescent sons, Christina's only grandchildren, Kade and Cyrus, and were supposed to have left four days ago. But because of the Christmas scare they are reluctant to leave, knowing the end is coming sooner than later, so they have extended their trip. Hence my bed-sharing with Joy. It's a good thing I'm a still and quiet sleeper. But then, how would I know? I live alone.

"I'll sleep anywhere, out on the veranda. I don't care. Family takes precedence."

"Yeah." Joy gives me a look. "But define family."

Christina has redecorated Don's old room and Joy has smudged it. It's been transformed since May. It is as though someone turned on a light in a dark place. Joy's things—trinkets and earrings and small containers and perfume and journal—sit on the right side of the double-wide, oversize bureau. She points to the empty left half. "That's your side." Joy is organized far beyond the average person. She is even organized more than the average *organized* person.

Joy keeps talking as she heads to the porch off her bedroom. She wants a cigarette and has been waiting with bated breath for me to arrive with a couple of packs of her special U.S. brand. She texted me two days before my flight, pleading with me to find some and rescue her from the horrible Mexican cigarettes she'd been forced to smoke after running out of her cherished American Spirit Light Green Mild. It was quite a feat to find them in Toronto. We are recovering smokers, but, well, our friend is dying, and we're both using that as a valid rationalization to smoke. The mind of an addict. I retrieve a pack from my bag and hand it to her.

"Oh, man. Thank you so much." She smacks it upside down on her left palm, tears the cellophane off, and opens the pack. She does all of this quickly, urgently. When she lights that first cigarette and inhales, she sighs in satisfaction. "Oh, yeah . . . that tastes great. *Thank* you." She takes another drag. "Thank you *so* much." *Woohoo!* She may not be bouncing on the outside, but she is on the inside.

I notice the earrings she's wearing. They're aqua and they dangle. "I like your earrings," I remark.

Joy raises her thumb and finger to one ear, and rubs

one of the earrings. "Oh, yeah. Me, too. They're a gift from Christina. We were going through her bedroom closet and all her jewelry. She's giving away a lot of her stuff. She gave these to me." I'll bet she put something aside for me, I think to myself. At least, I hope she did.

Note to self: remember, expectations are disappointments ordered in advance.

Joy grabs a small calendar off the bureau and begins to detail the plan. "So, here's the thing. You're bunking with me until Monday, then you go downstairs to El Rio until Friday, then you're back up here with me. That's when other guests arrive for the week. A family from Idaho. A friend of Nate's Christina helped raise and his kids. They've got the whole downstairs Monday through Friday."

Joy's got a pen in her hand, and she makes little stabbing motions at the tiny square boxes comprising the days of the month.

"Then, when *they* leave, you go back down to El Rio until *you* leave." She chuckles. "It's a turnstile of people right now. After the Christmas scare, people are beginning to get it. This is it, man. Last chance to see her."

"Yeah, but I knew that back in August when I booked this trip." There's an ugly little piece of me that resents getting bumped around.

"Yeah, but you're not people, you're *family.*" Joy says this easily, as if she had just declared it was daytime, and that it was obvious. *Whoosh.* The sound of my petty thinking slinking away and exiting stage left.

After the calendar review, Joy and I catch up and share another smoke. Her phone dings. It's WhatsApp, the electronic tissue connecting Joy, Christina, and all who want to communicate with either of them.

She picks up her phone and reads the message. "She's awake," Joy says as she stubs out the cigarette. "Let's go." It's back to the business of tasks. Joy is all about tasks and efficiency. She turns and heads toward the bedroom door. "And the dogs need to be let outside."

"Hey," I whisper softly as I creep around the corner of Christina's bedroom door. Her bed is to the right, the bathroom is to the left, and the mountains outside the veranda doors spread everywhere.

"Hey!" Christina turns to her left, toward me, stretches her arms up from her semi reclining position and we embrace.

Bella, Christina's rescue dog, stretches on the top of the bed. Her wiry black body, all twenty-two pounds of it, begins shaking back and forth in opposition to her tail, which whips wildly in welcome. Beware the tail—it'll take you out. Bella is Christina's constant companion. She doesn't leave the bed and must be carried outside to relieve herself on Christina's bad days. On the good days, Bella will hop down, scratch the bedroom door and ask to go out. Today is less than a good day, but better than a bad one. Bella stays put.

"*So* glad you're here," Christina says.

"Oh, Christina," I say through my hug, "it's so good to be here, so good to see you."

That's a white lie. What I mean is that it's good to be here *with* her, but it doesn't feel good to *see* her. Not at all. She looks so different—wasted, her eyes sunken, her limbs shriveled—so far from the firm, fierce Christina I've always known.

It's been seven months since I last saw her in person. I've seen photos posted on Facebook reflecting her decline, but I am completely unprepared for the extent of her physical deterioration. She has aged twenty years.

Her hair is thinner and longer and slightly unkempt, as though it hasn't been cut in a while. It looks the way the hair of an exhausted mother looks when she's been up three nights in a row with a sick child. Perpetual bedhead. Her arms and legs are skin-covered bones, emaciated, the muscles atrophied in a full-fledged retreat from life. She has lost forty pounds. She is still tan, but it has been two months since she's been able to get down to the pool. And it's been weeks since she ventured upstairs to the kitchen. Steps are beyond her capacity now. But she can, on her good days, still shuffle from her bed to the southern veranda eight steps away, slowly lower herself into a deck chair, and gaze out over the tiny town she has spent the past fifteen years nurturing.

She has invested all of herself into Boca. She has stared across the river to the mountains beyond from her bedroom for fifteen years. Every morning upon awaking, and every night upon retiring, those mountains are there, a steady, reassuring, unchanging natural vista. A visual reminder of the permanence of things. The view is her blankie, her cherished comfort-instilling constant. And now, she knows she will be relinquishing it, handing it over to the Great Unknown, and transitioning into impermanence herself.

"I'm *so* glad you're here," she repeats, smiling broadly.

What will I do once that smile is gone? I think to myself. How will I transition, release the reliability of her smile, her role in my life? Who will be my buoy now?

13

TASKS AND TIGHTNESS

Isabel, Casa la Ventana's devoted housekeeper, has brought Christina a new bottle of water, removed the top, popped in a straw, and placed it on the bedside table. When Christina reaches for it, the force of her grip causes the flimsy twelve-ounce plastic bottle to contract, and a bit of water is squeezed up and out of the bottle. Christina puts it back down while I get up to retrieve a paper towel.

"Do you want me to get you one of the big plastic cups from upstairs?" I ask. "Why do you use those anyway? The plastic and all."

"Yeah, I know, but Joy likes to know my water intake, and she measures by the bottles."

"Got it," I say over my shoulder from her bathroom.

"It's the little things," she says, apropos of nothing, when I return. "Joy knows about the little things." She takes the paper towel from my outstretched hand and dabs at the collar of her nightgown. "She always pours out the top inch of a new bottle, so it won't do this, spill water. Isabel doesn't think to do that."

Later, I think about *little* things, of how important

they are. That not having big things to contribute doesn't make the little things you *can* contribute any less valuable or appreciated. But in order to contribute little things, one must notice those little things, and become aware of them.

I am here, I am sure, to contribute some little thing, if only I knew what it is.

~

Christina wants the closet under the main stairway cleaned out and organized. A perfect job for Joy and her friend and fellow yoga devotee, Alesia, who has come to lend her grounded Mother Earth energy to the household. All of Joy's best friends—her posse—have met Christina and adore her. They are eager to provide whatever support they can during this challenging time. Alesia is here as much for Joy as for Christina. The constant *casa* cleaning up and clearing out process, coupled with the all-consuming caretaking duties are taking their toll on Joy. She is always pleasant and cheerful, but it's forced, in a way, sometimes. It reveals her anxiety to those who know her well.

Alesia is all rounded softness, clear skin, and warm, brown eyes. The mother of two children, her shape belies her depth of flexibility and strength of spirit. She loves to bake, and fortunately, is excellent at it. There is nothing worse than someone who comfort bakes for a grieving household only to produce dried out or undercooked products worthy of the dogs' less discriminating pallets. Alesia bakes fresh breakfast breads for Christina—blueberry, apple, carrot—coaxing her to eat a few bites.

Joy and I require no coaxing. Hot coffee and a hunk of freshly baked sweetbread is our idea of a great way to start our day. Neither of us is particularly a morning person, though I'm better at it than Joy. She's been in the hospitality industry for over twenty years, has no children or husband, and prefers to sleep until late morning. Now, she sets her alarm for eight o'clock in the morning, takes the dogs from Christina's bedroom to relieve themselves outside, smokes a cigarette, herds the dogs back inside for breakfast, and then heads back to bed. She does this mostly in quiet with a pinched, half-lidded look on her face. She's definitely not someone you want to chirp at in the morning; she'll give you a dead stare. What with the spiked hair and dead eyes and downturned mouth, most people give her a wide berth when she first awakens. You've got to let her have a cup of coffee before talking to her.

She arrived in November to visit for two weeks, and never left. Christina pretty much talked her into staying, though it hardly took much convincing as Christina considers Joy her adopted daughter. They even look like they could be related, both with short blonde hair, bright smiles, and blue eyes, though Joy lacks Christina's height.

Joy has put her life on hold until the end, whenever that comes. Her employer and the service staff at the restaurant in Colorado Springs where she has been a manager for years are all supporting her to take whatever time is needed. Her friends are caring for her dog and handling paperwork and bills, sending the clothes she needs, and the missing articles she saw no point in bringing on a short trip, but that for a long stay are like comfort food for the soul: her special sweatshirt, precious books, and her journal.

It's been several years since I spent any time with Joy, and I can see and feel the tightness in her. This is new. I have never known Joy to be anything other than light, airy, and effusive. Open, loving, carefree. The essence of upbeat. She is all those things, still, but the tightness shows through. She is on alert all the time now. There is a schedule, and a plan, and responsibilities. She has taken on the running of the house as well as tending to Christina. She covers the pool at night and turns off the pump, makes trips to the *tiendas* to purchase supplies, and interacts with the various service men and women who take care of the place. From the guy who trims the trees to the guy who sprays the perimeter of the house to prevent creepy crawly things from entering *la casa*. From the housekeeper, Isabel, to the groundskeeper, Toto, to all the others in between—the veterinarian, the doctors, nurses, townsfolk, and friends—Joy is now the middle-man, the go-between, the caretaker. She is intentionally walking into the shadow of death with her adopted Mexican momma, as she affectionately calls Christina, hand in hand, head held high. And she is prepared for the journey, having walked the last four months of her father's life when he, too, succumbed to cancer in 2015.

Joy is the last child of Joan, an artist, and Jim Wiggins, a stand-up comedian. She was their fifth and final child, and their sole daughter. She was cherished from the time she was born. But life wasn't easy for her with her dad on the road and then the death of her mother when she was nine years old. Only a few years after my sister, Jenny, and Joy's brother, Joe, married, Jim asked them to look after Joy and her teenage brother Josh. They all realized Jim needed to be back on the road after mourning his wife. They tried their best, as twenty-somethings, to ride herd on a couple of teenagers, but it was a challenging time for them all. Joy learned independence early—she had to.

Her dad was seventy-three years old when he died four years ago. He was a good friend of George Carlin's. George and Jim both wrote for the *Late Show with David*

Letterman back in the seventies. But George made it big and Jim didn't, though his final achievement was to land a guest spot on *The Tonight Show*, almost forty years later, and his routine was brilliant. Dressed in his signature black jeans and shirt against which his long white hair both accentuated his age while at the same time making him seem younger and hip, he stuck the landing. He brought down the house. He dubbed himself *a saloon comic* performer who openly smoked marijuana long before any state or country had legalized it. He was the comic's Willie Nelson. He mentored many young comics. He appeared on *Last Comic Standing* and should have won —everyone on the show acknowledged it—but for TV ratings and nepotistic political reasons, someone else took home the prize.

One of his best sets had to do with pooping. He would declare that at his age—in his late fifties at the time—having a good poop in the morning was a pleasure with better odds than having sex at night. He sold merchandise in the back of the room after he finished his act, as most performers do—they make as much or more on merchandise than they do on their performance—and his best-selling item, hands down, was a baseball hat and a T-shirt, the front of which read "Have you pooped today?" He used to wear the hat on stage, a lit cigarette in one hand and a shot of tequila in the other. He was full of life until the cancer diagnosis. When he became ill and it became clear he was wrapping up his last show, Joy dropped her life in Colorado and moved to Wisconsin to care for her dad the last four months of his life. It's who she is, it's what she does.

Joy was born for this role, that of caretaker, note writer, list maker. She organizes and cleans. Everything. Her OCD is a real plus in the end stages of life: disinfecting doorknobs, scrubbing counter corners, organizing closets, measuring out medications. She decided long ago not to marry or have children of her own, but she is the favorite aunt of all her friends' kids, and the constant rescuer of abandoned animals. Joy's name is an apt one; it emanates from her.

I remember once, years ago, I visited her in Colorado Springs for an overnight while traveling somewhere. This was before the days of easy ATM access and I found myself out of cash. I needed twenty dollars for some reason or another. Without a second's hesitation, Joy whipped out a twenty dollar bill from her pocket and smiled brightly.

"Here," she chirped. "I've got a twenty. Take it—it's yours!" Years later, I found out that was all she had at the time and had to wait until her next paycheck for some cash. It humbled me. Generous Joy. That's who she is.

But she is also bit of a paradox. She, like many survivors of early emotional trauma and loss, veers from commitment out of a fear of abandonment. She's witnessed and internalized the fragility of the physical, the echo in the emotional. It has made her stronger and more determined, to be sure, but also more cautious when it comes to commitment in romantic relationships. But, when it comes to her brothers, or her chosen sisters, or her work family, or her adopted Mexican momma, Joy is all in, all the time, with caution cast to the wind and fragility flung far away. She is a little warrior. A little love warrior, marching toward her momma's certain end, uncertain of the way, but committed to completing the journey.

14

LAPTOPS, LOVE, AND LOSS

I've had a MacBook Air laptop, an eleven-inch version, since it first came out. It's my tried and true travel companion. It fits in my traveling shoulder bag perfectly. While I don't make my living by writing, I do a lot of it in order to earn a living. I adore writing. I love everything about it, even when it's hard, even when it's an utter slog to produce two hundred decent words in one sitting. Not only do I enjoy the actual process of writing—rooting through the language landscape like a truffle-sniffing pig in search of the perfect word—I find it immensely therapeutic. I've hammered out some steely pain in my time.

At the base of this love of the written word is a love of reading, instilled by my parents, as well as a respect for words themselves, also a gift from my parents, and one supported by my schooling. I'm old enough to have studied Latin, back when it was a mandatory subject at the girls school I attended. I thought it a silly waste of time to study a dead language when I was fourteen, but long after I graduated, I continue to bless the fact that learning it was once required of me.

Language matters. Words matter. The landscape of language we now occupy—we as a people, as a species—is too often one of hate and division. Christina and I talk about this regularly. Almost every conversation refers to or mentions the ill effects of the current U.S. administration, the uptick in violence in behavior and language, the loss of decorum and civility in politics, the denial and dismissal of scientific fact-based research regarding climate change. I fear we may have already screwed things up so badly that my grandson, when he becomes my age or well before, will have to retreat to the woods in order to survive. That is, if there are any woods left.

Knowing that this would most likely be my last visit ever with Christina, I intended to chronicle all of my terribly important thoughts and feelings about it and whatever memories we might make this time, our last together in this lifetime. And I had my trusty laptop along with me to aid in that endeavor. I would capture it in the moment, as it happened, like folding laundry fresh from the dryer. I would write big thoughts, deep thoughts. Oh, the plans I had! God must have been doubled over in laughter, because within a few days my trusty laptop bit the dust. It started as a small cough, then erratic spasms, until it finally crashed.

Finding an Apple doctor is not easy in Puerto Vallarta, nor is my ability to find patience while feeling powerless.

This is the first time I have been without my laptop in the last decade. Given that it sank into a coma on a Friday afternoon exactly one week after my arrival, my second Friday, I can't even begin to attend to it until Monday. I can feel the early warning signs of impending panic. Withdrawal symptoms. *Fuck!*

I feel compelled to add that my technical knowledge of all things electric, computers and the like, is rather limited. That's a lie, it sucks. I'm light-years behind my sons. I get by, but barely. I know what a plug is, where to put it, and why it's necessary. I know how to open Microsoft Word. I sort of almost understand Power-Point. I have no clue about modems and DVD players and Bose wireless speakers. I have no clue about anything wireless, period. I'm still trying to *grok* the relationship between wifi and data on my phone. I pray a lot when it comes to my electronics. Gadgets change too quickly for me these days. Somehow, somewhere after the cassette tape fell out of favor, I got lost. The world veered toward CD and then sprinted to Spotify and I got stuck in the electronic shuffle. I own an iPhone, primarily so I can FaceTime with my grandchildren and my sons, but I consistently forget to take it with me when leaving for an appointment, which is an indication of its lack of significance in my life. I do not read on it. I do not play games on it, take notes on it, or depend on it. But my laptop? My laptop is different. I am completely, utterly, hopelessly dependent upon it to express myself, run my business, and connect to and communicate with the world at large. I love my laptop. No, really. I *love* it. Too much, I think.

I go whine to Christina, and fortunately, she finds a guy online from a northern section of Puerto Vallarta who comes highly recommended, has a Facebook page with lots of great reviews, and most important of all, speaks English. Speaks English *and* specializes in Apple products. That's enough for me. I call. For a few thousand pesos or approximately fifty dollars U.S., Israel says he will make the trip to Boca and diagnose the damage to my baby. When can he do this? Tonight. At 7:00 p.m. on a Friday night he's willing to make a house call. Seriously? I think I love this guy.

Israel arrives a couple of hours later, examines my

baby, and then takes it apart. It's scary to watch, at least for me. After much exploration and many wires attached to things I don't understand nor care to, he determines it's the command key; it's gotten stuck and cannot be repaired, so I need a new keyboard. It's a two-year old computer. They don't build things like they used to.

This was *so* not a part of my plan. I'm thinking of the agony of parting with my laptop for at least a week, if not longer. Israel tells me he can't get to it until Monday, but he can order the part. He should be done by Tuesday night. He can deliver it back to me Wednesday evening after work! I feel relief flood my body. My baby has a diagnosis and a treatment plan! I begin to believe I can survive for five days until its return.

The next day, I head down the stairs and over the bridge to pick up a couple of things from the *tienda*. I hear my name being called as I walk the dusty road in front of the clinic. *"Ceentia."* It must be someone local; they're the only ones who draw out the *e* sound like that. I stop and look around me for the source. I am about halfway between the bridge to the south side of the river where Christina lives, and the beach at the west end of the street, where boats wait to be loaded with building supplies. This is where the workmen come and go, loading their sturdy little vessels with materials to be delivered to various water access work sites. It's the *burro* watering hole. I recognize few, if any, of the current workmen gathered there. I hear my name called again, and finally find the source. Chapa waves from the sandy ramp, water up to his calves. He leaves the side of the boat he's filling and trots toward me.

"Chapa!" I am delighted to see him. It's been at least five years since our paths have crossed. He used to work for Christina, as did his wife. He tended the outside, she the inside. Chapa helped carve the gardens from the mountainside, placing bricks and building walls and bringing all manner of rare indigenous plants and trees, as well as all kinds of orchids, back from his hikes deep into the forest. Chapa built the large decorative wall opposite the retaining wall by the pool. He has no training, no schooling. But he has four children and has carved out a living in this tiny town in the same way he cultivated Christina's gardens over the years, with patience and ingenuity and a strong back.

Then, a rift opened between his wife and Christina and it spilled out and over onto Chapa, who wanted — and tried — to stay out of it, but to no avail. Eventually, for his personal sanity, not to mention his safety, Chapa had to quit after his wife was fired for stealing from a guest. Had she admitted it, had she apologized, Christina would have bent over backward to address the underlying cause for that kind of behavior, but Chapa's wife wouldn't and so that was that. Broke Christina's heart. And Chapa's.

But he is all smiles as he walks toward me. I move quickly toward him, too, and we meet in a big bear hug, him all sweaty, and me not caring. Chapa's smile could light up a dark cathedral. Ear-to-ear, his smile runs. Big, straight white teeth beaming from an indigenously dark face topped with still-black hair. He doesn't look a day older than when I saw him last, despite the fact that we are both grandparents now, and there is the beginning of grey at his temples. I had heard he had begun drinking again, something he had forsaken for years, but he appears bright-eyed and healthy this day. And he is happy to see me, genuinely happy. We converse as we always did, easily, me slipping into my pidgin Spanish and handy-dandy charade skills, him translating. *Como se dice* is my favorite phrase.

He has gotten a new job taking care of a big house on

the south side of the river. He says they treat him well, that he likes it. I ask if he's seen Christina recently. He lowers his gaze to the sand beneath his bare feet and shakes his head. He knows about the cancer. "Esta no bueno," he says. He shakes his head again. The mention of cancer loops in Silvia, Toto's mother, whose death two years ago left a bit of a hole inside the town's heart.

It occurs to me as we part that if this happens to be the last time I ever see Chapa, seeing as how I'm back playing the game that I, too, have a known stale date, I would be glad for this particular exchange. If I never saw him again, I would feel complete, and that's a good feeling. Because you never know. I didn't have that with Silvia, a chance to say goodbye, to voice my gratitude for having been accepted into her family all those years ago. I had been unmoored, and she had provided a welcome harbor.

It's important to notice an opportunity to make an interaction you have with someone be kind, as if it were the last one you might have with them—because it might be. Life is like that; like the classic card game of Gin, it'll cover the completion card if you don't pick it up off the discard pile when given the chance.

15

HOVERING TAKES HOLD

For the first few days, I hover outside Christina's bedroom door, wondering if she's awake. I peek around the corner. Sometimes, many times, she has her eyes closed and her head to one side. Other times, she's on the phone or scrolling through her social media feeds, replying to well-wishers. She stays in constant communication with others during this time of deterioration, firmly establishing boundaries with those she may not wish to see or talk to. Even listening tires her. But she loves to play the internet game Words with Friends, which requires no listening or talking. She takes particular delight in trouncing a worthy competitor with a seven-letter word. "Ha! How do you like *them* apples?"

I feel the need, increasingly, to try and make sense of the tightrope I'm walking. Emotional eggshells. I want to be with her, but I don't want to intrude. And I don't want to tire her by sitting bedside all day, chirping at her, getting underfoot. I wouldn't want someone staring at me all the time, watching me wither away. But then, what am I to *do*? What *can* I do, save stand watch and preserve the quiet when Joy goes to town, as she has this morning?

I feel off balance. I don't know where I fit in, where my place is, what my role is. I feel like a mere visitor, at arm's length, an observer, and I find *that* role unsatisfying and unsettling. I want to participate, to contribute. I want to *do* something, dammit. I am accustomed to occupying a position of at least *some* authority, of having a place at the table, and a voice. I seem to have lost all three. I feel removed from Christina and I don't know if it's me or her. She *invited* me. She says she wants me here, but I don't *feel* it. I can't help feeling as though I'm intruding somehow. The warmth and closeness of our May visit feels distant and distorted. So, I hover around her door and wait for slivers of time and glimpses of attention. Joy, however, strides right into Christina's room. She walks into her room whenever she wants, sticks her head around the door and says, "Hey—how you doing?"

I observe Joy's smooth interactions with Christina. They seem effortless, practiced. I observe their familiarity with something akin to envy. I understand, intellectually, that this dance they are doing is one of necessity. Born out of love, yes, and perpetuated by devotion, to be sure, but a dance dictated by need. The need to deal with the pain. The need to deal with Christina's imminent death, and keep track of the pills, the appointments, the house, and the animals. All the details Christina holds in her head about the upkeep and running of Casa la Ventana must be downloaded before she dies, and Joy is the recipient. It is a delicate dance with a myriad of steps, and not only do I not want to step on any toes, I'm not sure I want to learn the dance.

There is an urgency to Christina's energy that I have not experienced before. She has things she wants to accomplish. In over thirty years, I've never seen her display anything close to the freneticism emanating from her now, even when under extreme stress. She's the very definition of calm in crisis. But, she's running out of time and she knows it. The pain is her daily reminder of how little time remains. The *tick-tock* of time is measured in medications.

She and Joy have one purpose each day, and one purpose only: to stay ahead of the pain. It is their guiding light, their North Star. Get through the day on schedule, with the pain below a five on a scale of one to ten. When they fall behind—through human forgetfulness or physical interruption—and the pain flairs up and grips her, Christina's answers and requests become short. Her speech becomes clipped and lacks warmth. She gets right to the point. That scalpel again. She becomes irritable and demanding. She wants what she wants, and she wants it *now*. Much of this is due to the medications and their side effects, but mostly it's due to the increasing pain and the decreasing time it reflects.

Everyone around her understands what's going on— we all respond quickly, though sometimes our actions are accompanied by a raised eyebrow or subtle sigh—it's just that it's such a departure from the way she *was*, back when things were normal. Back when she didn't know her stale date and we didn't know she had one. Back when none of us knew she wouldn't be here in a few months. Or weeks. The not knowing, the uncertainty, underlies and exacerbates the tension. Learning to navigate that sea of uncertainty requires a massive amount of trust, which in turn demands a certain degree of surrender.

So, when she makes a specific, direct request of me, I jump at the chance to fulfill it. Reading is too tiring for her now, requiring more focus than she can give, so she has taken to listening to audio books. She asks me to read Dr. Brian Weiss' book, *Many Lives, Many Masters*, a book which had a profound impact on me when I first read it in 1993. That was the moment I first considered the notion of reincarnation, which had not been part of my Christian upbringing. Employing the lens of past lives has changed the way I experience my current one.

And now she wants me to read *that* book to her? She wants me to read a book that altered my view of the world and my life within it out loud to my big sister? *That* I can do, I think to myself, and do well. I have found my place at the table, my voice. I feel almost giddy when I go to bed that night, as though it's Christmas Eve. I have a role, something to *do*, a way to *contribute*.

16

PUT IT ON THE LIST

L eo stops by to get the shopping list.
       Leo is a go-to kind of guy. He's dependable but approaches life with an air of disdain and distance. He only trusts a few people. Christina is one of them. But his arm's length attitude is balanced by his devotion; once he trusts you, he's there for you.

Leo drives into Vallarta once a week, usually on Tuesdays, to Costco and any other place on Christina's list. It's how he helps. He likes a schedule and sticks to it, or tries to, when people aren't slowing him down, or asking him questions, or being indecisive. And lists, he likes lists. Joy makes them for him, writing everything down in legible elementary-style printing. In response to my verbal request for him to please grab some chocolate for me, he says, "Put it on the list. If it ain't on the list, it don't get bought." For Leo, if it ain't in black and white, it ain't real. Grey makes him nervous.

Leo lives further down the north side of the river along the dirt path that runs from the footbridge to the ocean. He lives in a second story two-bedroom apartment right where the river meets the ocean. His front door is an imposing steel plate at the end of a small, dank concrete stairway. Not a shred of an aesthetic sense exists there, not a plant nor any other visible sign of even an *attempt* at prettying up the entrance, which could desperately use it. There isn't a woman's touch within ten yards of Leo's place.

He pours his first drink at 5:00 p.m, makes sure there's plenty of ice in his freezer, and waits until 7:00 p.m. each evening before lighting his daily joint. He fought in Vietnam twice and was the first person to serve two tours, though other soldiers followed. Afterwards, seeking a less stressful life, he, like Christina, replanted himself in southern soil. He made a plan, saved his money, sold all his stuff, and moved to Boca de Tomatlán, to his steel door and blackened bedroom window. Leo likes to control his environment and he is, to put it politely, a private person.

He is also a mighty mangler of the English language. *Regurgitating* might come out as "he was *re-gigurgitating* all over the place!" He gets to the point on all things and can't stand bullshit or small talk. He also doesn't relish people jabbering at him, especially if someone is asking unnecessary questions. That constitutes jabbering. But his heart is as big as his chest and Christina owns a large part of it. They've known each other since she and Don moved here. Their friendship took root as she built Casa la Ventana. For years, Christina cut Leo's hair. She was good with a pair of scissors. For Leo, that was the ultimate intimacy, him letting her cut his hair. It took a long time for him to take her up on her offer. Now, she can no longer wield a pair of shears.

Friendship is built one step at a time, and ascends that way, too, just like Christina's 101 steps, which are becoming more painful for Leo to climb. He needs a new hip and has already scheduled replacement surgery in Puerto Vallarta for February 24ᵗʰ. He has arranged care for the first few days and after that says he'll be fine. He has a plan and a schedule and his lists.

"Bone on bone," he replies when I ask him how the pain is. He draws it out while holding my gaze. It comes out sounding like *baowwwwnnn*.

"Ew." Physically flinching at the thought of the pain, I make the lemon face one makes in the face of the gruesome. I've experienced bone on bone pain. It ain't fun.

Leo stares at me from the big leather recliner a few feet from Christina's bed while he awaits last-minute list additions. Joy and Christina discuss the additions in the background. I stand at the door, leaning. It's where I hang when people are there. I'm on the fringe. Like a hovercraft, I just stand there, waiting for something to *do*.

"Not many people I'd climb these goddamn steps for," he says. He leans forward in the chair, tilts himself toward me, and lowers his voice before continuing, as though it's a secret.

"Want to know how many?"

I nod, smile, and play along, but I know the punch line in advance.

"One." He raises his right index finger to emphasize. "One," he repeats, drawing it out like he had with *bone*. Originally from Delaware, his accent is a mixture of Baltimore and Philadelphia, with more pronounced *o* sounds. I smile and nod in response. Leo leans back in the chair. In preparation for knee replacement surgery, he has lost twenty-five pounds since I saw him in May. He had been carrying a bit of gut. It's gone now. He's still a big old bear, but one that a new hip can more readily carry forward into to a less painful future.

Joy finally turns and thrusts the list at Leo. "Done." She reviews it with him to ensure he can read everything. And then he's off, Christina's over-size insulated bags in hand, to the great and powerful land of Costco. He will waste no time on this trip, since he's traveling alone for a change. Leo likes no one *jabbering* at him or diverting him from his schedule.

I am quite fond of Leo. He's good people and has been a true friend to Christina. I hope his new hip is as good to him.

Christina's appetite has shrunk in inverse proportion to her pain. Getting her to eat is becoming increasingly difficult. We measure in bites now. Every other day, when she shuffles to her shower, she weighs herself on the scale. Last check she was down to 119 pounds. That's on the frame of a woman who was once five-foot-ten and over 160 pounds of toned muscle. She lived a healthy lifestyle. She walked up and down countless steps every day. Who needs a Fitbit when you live on the side of a mountain? Now, her height has shrunk, too; she's lost three inches. She weighs less than I do. Her skin hangs from her diminished frame.

So, everyone is happy when Christina requests a BLT sandwich. It means her appetite has improved a little, at least on this day, which happens to be another Tuesday and Leo is heading into the big city for supplies. Christina is becoming become quite focused in her desires. Specific. She wants a certain kind of bacon. She asks Joy to add bacon to the shopping list for Leo. More specifically, she wants bacon from *Costco*. They carry the thick cut three-pack bacon she likes. Joy is a vegetarian who refuses to touch meat, so it has been awhile since

Christina tasted bacon. It's been since her son and his family—who have no problem touching, cooking, or eating meat—left after the new year.

In addition, Christina wants her BLT to be made with a fresh croissant, again, from Costco. She does *not* want the ones from Mega, the local large grocery store. And fresh tomatoes, but not from Costco. She wants those from across the river, where they're fresher. I can almost feel Christina's anticipation. The fact that her appetite has returned, if only briefly, also lifts her mood, which lifts the mood of the entire household. Isabel and Toto can feel it. So can I. And Joy. Even the animals feel it. It's not that she moves from her bed, but the lilt of her voice and her laugh can be heard in the open-air space when her bedroom door is open. Today, her door is open to visitors, and her belly is open to food. It's a good day. She has her wits about her.

I know this because she's asked *me* to construct the BLT. I've made them for her before, many times. There's an art to achieving the necessary crunch factor of the bacon, a balance between crunchy and chewy, that's fundamental to the quality of the final product. She and I have actually discussed this before. I happen to be a bacon-cooking queen. So, Christina knows a) it's something I can do, and do well, and b) it gives me something useful to do so I'll stop hovering and asking her if she needs anything. It must be annoying to be asked so often by so many people who want so badly only to help, and have no response because underneath any response is the truth that nothing can help, not really, and not for long.

Plus, Christina knows I can't really cook much of anything. Well, not so much *can't*, as *don't*. It's not so much a lack of ability as it is simply a lack of desire. I do a few things well in the kitchen—I make a mean pot roast and leg of lamb—I just don't enjoy the cooking process much, though I enjoy the dining experience, the actual eating experience. I enjoy the ambience of a beautiful table setting, I enjoy going out and being served. I enjoy elegance and sophistication. I just don't enjoy the shopping for or preparation of food. I don't look for opportunities to express myself in that particular room of the house. It's not my bag. To me, in my own kitchen, food is fuel and eating dinner is a required pre-requisite to deserve dessert. In my world, chocolate is a basic food group and must be consumed daily for maximum well-being.

But, when Leo returns to Boca laden with the list's items, the bacon is not from Costco. He claims they didn't have it. Christina's eyes claim he didn't look hard enough. But he did get the proper croissants, and everything else, and some chocolate for me. All is forgiven. I can make do with thin cut. I will simply use more bacon per sandwich. Bacon is bacon, whether thick or thin cut, and with a certified bacon master manning the pan, a quality BLT will be coming forthwith.

One thing about Christina's kitchen: she's got this monster of a gas stove. It's a professional six-burner for people who care about cooking. A bomb could go off and this thing would survive. It's a huge, hulking iron beast of imposing proportions that weighs a ton. Literally. How on earth they got that sucker over the bridge, up the path, and then up 101 stairs without any machinery is beyond me. When I once asked her how on earth it was managed, Christina had replied, "Many Mexican men." And she cooked for all of them, those that built her house, and the many who came after to assist in her constant refinements. Christina loves to cook and is quite the perfectionist with certain recipes. But, she'll experiment, too, and frequently creates new dishes. Her spontaneity shines in the kitchen. We have had our own well-practiced dance when dining together. She cooks and I set the table and create the ambience, two sides of the dining experience.

I crank up the stove and start in on the bacon. As I said, it's an art and it can't be rushed. Also, the slicing of the tomato must be thin, thin, thin, and the lettuce folded and placed just so. The perfect amount of mayonnaise must be spread to the very edges of the croissant. Chips and pickles are placed on the side. It's the little things; quality is defined by and revealed through attention to details. Thirty-five minutes later, two expertly cooked, sturdily constructed and beautifully presented BLTs make their way downstairs to Christina's bedroom. She dives right in. I knew they'd taste good and that she'd enjoy them, but when she takes that first bite, her eyes close and she makes the sound people make when they sink into the deliciousness of what they're tasting, the Campbell's Soup *m'm m'm good* sound. A love grunt.

She chews the bite slowly, savoring it. Then she swallows, opens her eyes, turns to me, and smiles the kind of full-bodied smile that lights up a room.

"Perfect," she says. "Just perfect. So worth waiting for." She eyes her sandwich again, sighs, and says, "Thank you. I just love bacon." And then she eats the whole BLT while I watch. I'm smiling the entire time. My insides feel warm, as though I've made a considerable contribution that day. I made my friend something she wanted, something she appreciates, something that made her smile from the inside out.

The importance of a sense of purpose cannot be underestimated.

She finishes and thanks me again. I take her tray and head back to the kitchen. As I climb the stairs, I ask over my shoulder, "You want some ice cream?"

"Not now. I'm full. Maybe later."

I clear her tray and wash the plate. I wrap the remaining sandwich carefully and put it away for another day. Because maybe it'll be a good day tomorrow, too. Maybe it'll be an open-door day, a BLT day, a day with a purpose. And less pain.

17

ROUTINES

I am learning some of the routines, sinking into the rhythm and necessity of them. The little things. Like siphoning off the top inch of water in a new water bottle before handing it to Christina. Or like straightening the bedspread and fluffing the pillows before she returns from the bathroom. She sleeps on top of the bedspread with just a lightweight blanket on top of her. I'm not always there when she leaves the bed to make her way to the bathroom, but when I am, I take real pride in my bedspread straightening and tucking abilities, not to mention my pillow fluffing excellence. In order to accomplish the bedspread pulling, the bedside table must be moved away from the door and then shoved back into place tight against the freshly smoothed out bed. That keeps it in place longer. But the bedside table must to pushed up tightly against the bed, or else the door hits the corner of it. It's a tight fit.

It's the little things.

There's a special lotion she likes from Bath & Body Works. At her request I brought several tubes of it with me this trip. I'm learning how much to use and where to apply it. I watch Joy squeeze the cream from the tube into her palms, rubbing them together before reaching out to apply it to Christina's frail body. First her neck, then arms, then legs, beginning at the calves and working up, then down to the feet. Christina can reach her upper parts, not her legs, so Joy spends time on the calves and soles of Christina's feet. The lotion, of course, comes after the shower, which is a dance Christina and Joy do every other day: the plastic chair Christina sits in under the shower head, what gets handed to her and when while she washes herself, blow-drying her hair, applying a bit of lip gloss. The little things. Minor, but major at the same time. It's a delicate dance. And it's all a game of inches.

Come to think of it, so is life.

Christina and I talk politics on a regular basis, both of us fueled by our mutual disregard for the current U.S. administration. We are appalled by the apparent willful ignorance—which is how author and psychologist M. Scott Peck defines evil—of a certain percentage of the American citizenry, and the underlying fear that fuels their anger. I am both heartened and dismayed to know that throughout American history, one third of the American population was against abolishing slavery, a woman's right to vote, and the civil rights act, so it seems there is a certain percentage of people that don't like progressive, inclusive change.

The language of discord and division has overtaken the lexicon of the American landscape, spreading obfuscation. The language of pain has even seeped into our colloquialisms: *no pain, no gain, I love you to death, it can't hurt to try, I'm so happy I could just die!*

"He was a hurt little boy," Christina remarks about the President, her voice void of the vitriol usually reflected when his name is mentioned. "He grew to become a selfish, angry man. I feel sorry for him."

When I mention that's nice for her, but how about her grandsons, shouldn't she feel outraged on their behalf, given what we're doing to the planet and its resources?

"Frankly, I don't give a shit about any *shoulds* anymore." She laughs. "I just don't give a should." After a beat, "Besides, takes too much out of me to be angry. Takes too much out of me to be angry with anyone."

She's right. It does.

Shoulds suck.

~

It is 4:00 p.m. and the animals have begun their dinner dance.

What is it about animals that though they are fed at the exact same time every day, their internal clock goes off an hour before the customary time? Maya lays in the garden, under the table, at my feet. Should I move at all, in any small way—simply to cross my legs or lean back in the chair—her head snaps up off the ground and she's on alert. *Human in motion! Could be dinner time! Dinner time!*

"Maya, it is *not* dinner time. It is four o'clock. You have another hour. Go back to sleep."

I return to reading my book, and Maya's head lowers to the ground, between her outstretched paws, eyes open. She sighs. Christina's cat, Bruja, must run on the same time program because she appears from out of nowhere and sashays her way toward me. She must have been napping in the brush; she's covered in dust and bits of dried leaves. She begins rubbing my right calf in what I'm sure she thinks is a winsome way.

"Yeah, you want your dinner, too, eh, Miss Bruja?" I reach down and wipe her sleek black coat. "No such luck, sweetheart. You've got one more hour, too, just like Miss Maya. So, relax. Go lie down in the sun." Bruja seems to understand. She turns and wanders away from me, and then her tail goes tall and straight like a giant middle finger displaying her true feelings. She flops down in the sun about six feet away from my little table, only steps from the front portico. Cats are smart that way. Why hang at the feeder's feet when she'll head to the front door eventually? Proximity improves more immediate access.

Eventually, Bruja gets to be right. After another forty-five minutes of them watching me with their pleading eyes and silent, accusatory stares, I finally succumb to their telepathic angst and head inside. Maya is urgent in her desires, whimpering in grateful anticipation. Bruja, not so much. *It's about time*, she communicates as she passes us both, moving up the stairs toward the kitchen like black mercury in motion.

I hear Bella whine from behind Christina's closed door. She has the same internal alarm system as her furry friends but won't leave Christina's bed until someone comes and gets her. I open the door quietly—Christina is asleep—and Bella bounds out and up the stairs, a blur of kinetic energy. *Dinner! Dinner!* By the time I get to the kitchen, all three animals are in their assigned places, waiting with the same sort of patience demonstrated by children around the world on Christmas morning. *Now! Now! Now!*

Almost a decade ago, Maya became ill. She's had urinary tract infections and digestive issues since I've known her. Christina tried all sorts of things, from medications to special diets, but Maya would dribble all over the house, poor thing, and struggle mightily to poop. At one point, Christina considered a pricey operation, but ultimately decided she'd take on Maya's healing solo. After experimenting, she concocted a recipe that resulted in what would become all the animals' meals forever. Every weekend she would cook up a huge batch of food for Maya—a week's worth—in an equally enormous pot that contained chicken, rice, lentils, carrots, oats, and potatoes. She did not add preservatives, but included lots of healing herbs. The end result was a hearty, firm stew. When cooled, it was put it into two large containers and *viola!* The dogs had food for the week.

Maya got better and the food routine was set. The same food, morning and night, at the same time, in the same place, is served to the animals every day. When Bruja joined the family, she had no choice but to adopt the routine. Having been a feral cat, any food that was actually *served* to her was fine by her. She did, however, indicate her distaste for chicken, preferring tuna instead. Christina acquiesced to that, and so there is always at least a half a dozen cans of tuna on the pantry shelf.

After dishing out the prepared food—precise amounts in assigned dishes—I make the animals sit, (except Bruja, who communicates *fuck off* in response to any command of any kind), and they do, immediately, tails wagging wildly back and forth on the floor while I hold their dishes chest high. They know the drill. Maya gets her bowl set down first, next to the kitchen counter near the microwave. Bella sits three feet away, near the bathroom door. And, finally, Bruja, who is fed up, on the northern windowsill in the midst of Christina's live herb pots of thyme, basil, rosemary, and mint. Casa la Ventana is not a meritocracy; the pecking order is based entirely on seniority. Bella is okay with this. Bruja, not so much. She mews loudly at me from the time I place the dog dishes on the floor until the time I walk her dish over to the window and place her bowl on the ledge.

I stand there watching the mammals snarf down their food with grateful gusto. The clock reads 4:51. I hope I haven't blown the routine to bits, but more, I hope Joy doesn't ask me what time I fed them. It would present an ethical choice: tell the truth and suffer her withering glance, or lie and save my skin but lose a piece of my soul.

It occurs to me that giving in to the animals telepathic pleading nine minutes early is hardly a crime, but it does sort of smell a little like my son's issue with me, grand-parental disregard for parental boundaries. In my own defense, sometimes you don't know what the rules are until *after* you've broken them. "Um, Mom, we don't let him have *that*."

"Oh, sorry, I didn't know."

Early on, I spent a lot of time apologizing. Parenting has changed.

When I visited last year, Peyton and I watched YouTube videos in his bed one morning, horse videos, scenes from movies like *Secretariat* and *Sea Biscuit*. Peyton had developed a thing for horses, and it was a delicious experience to snuggle with him and share in his delight.

"One more, CC," he said when one video ended after three minutes. "Please."

"Okay. One more, Peyton. One." He was learning his numbers and how to count.

"One," he repeated and then raised his tiny index finger as well, his eyebrows lowering slightly, indicating his understanding, and the seriousness of his intent.

My heart melted right there. *I never did this kind of thing with my kids when they were little boys*, I think to

myself. *At least, I don't remember doing it. Too busy, I guess.*
And so, we watched one more. Twenty times we watched
one more. For two weeks after I left, every morning, that
devil child would wake up and ask his parents if he could
watch horse videos. *Dammit!* My son gave me a stern
talking to later. "No more videos on the laptop. It's not
that you can't do it, but we've got to put controls on it
now, Mom. It's hard to be the ones to have to say *no*
twenty times first thing every morning. It's not a fun way
to start the day."

I hadn't considered the flip side to my pleasure, my
son's pain.

Now, when I visit, Peyton and I watch horse videos
on the big screen TV, and *only* on weekends, and *only*
with parental permission. I'm good with that. It's not
about me, it's about boundaries and routines and safe
parameters of participation for Peyton. I mean, nobody
told us that watching snippets of horse movies was a
potentially detrimental thing, because it *wasn't*. It became
counterproductive with the *one more* thing, which is
completely on me; I didn't want to say no to him. And
that's how some routines become harmful routines,
because they protect us from the pain of *something*,
whether it's hunger, or cold, or digestive issues, or horse
videos. Routines take root in pain of some kind. They
exist to keep pain out, like chicken wire exists around a
hen house to prevent a fox from entering.

And it occurs to me, now, while watching these
hungry animals lick their bowls clean, that there's something important here, some sort of truth that might also
be inconvenient. I know, at least intellectually, that my
son is absolutely correct. And I want to adhere to his
wishes (read rules). Really, I do. But emotionally? I'm
kind of like Bruja. *Read my tail.* It might be an eldest child
kind of hubris. Or, maybe it's my own peculiar brand of

it, a need to get away with something. My neural path-
ways were forged in the fire of an alcoholic household.
Secrets and special and all that crap all wrapped
together. Suddenly, I see Peyton in my mind's eye. He's
twelve and pleading for *one more, CC!*

Codependency is the gift that keeps on giving.

As I retrieve the now empty dog bowls and wash
them out—part of the routine—I vow to myself that
tomorrow I will *not* succumb to Maya's telepathic
torture. I will adhere to the routine! I *will* follow the
rules, dammit!

God, I hope I haven't screwed up my grandson for
life.

18

ICE CREAM IS GOOD FOR
THE SOUL

J oy and Alesia have gone in search of coconut ice cream at the new store across the river. They return having had a bite to eat and a bit to drink. They are in good spirits. Joy bounds into Christina's room where I sit in the leather recliner. She holds four ice cream bars in her left hand.

"No coconut, but these are lemon ice bars. Want one?"

"Maybe later. Thanks." Christina is tired. It's in her eyes. Feigned *thank you* smiles cannot cover the lack of life force energy. Joy sees it, too, and finishes her report.

"They were out of Agua de Jamaica juice. But I ordered five bottles. They'll be here Tuesday, and I'll pick them up when I get back from town with Leo."

"Okay. Great, thanks." Christina slowly lifts herself up a bit on her bed with her increasingly sticklike arms. She is concentrating, focused on the effort required to make such a slight movement. "Where did you eat?" she asks.

"At Ramones. We had fish tacos. I brought a couple back. Want one?"

"No, I'm not hungry, thanks."

"Okay. I'll put it in the fridge for later." Joy turns around to leave but then turns back. "Oh, and I got hit on by a really ugly Mexican guy. That was fun." Joy means the opposite. She is used to getting hit on; her bubbly personality wrapped in a cute, compact package reels them in on a regular basis. When Joy walks down a street, it's like throwing chum in the ocean. Men of all shapes and sizes and ages and ethnicities appear from out of nowhere. She can't help it. It's not that she flirts with them, it's that she flirts with life, and that's seductive— and contagious.

"Was it the same guy as yesterday?"

"No, different guy. Same creep factor, though." She pauses. "So, how are you?"

"I took a pill, a red one." Christina's eyes are closed.

"At seven," I chime in. Joy likes to know times and I want so badly to be helpful. She likes to know days and times and pills and when they were taken and what was eaten and when it came out. Pooping is a major item of interest. Joy keeps meticulous notes. Everything is written down in a small spiral-bound notebook.

"What?" Joy almost does a double take. She looks at me, her expression chastising me for allowing this off schedule pill popping to occur. She turns her disap- proving eye back to Christina.

"You had one right before your treatment. That was around five o'clock." She looks up and away for a moment, remembering. She's checking her internal clock. "Yeah, I was feeding the dogs." It is an understood household rule. Don't mess with the schedule. It's there for everyone's safety and sanity.

"Oh, well," Christina says with a small grin and a wave of her hand. "I guess I screwed *that* up." She knows about the schedules. She also knows which ones

are important and which ones aren't, and which ones
become obsolete in the face of pain. Plans can be super-
seded in a second. She starts coughing. The phlegm is
thick but loose and she reaches for her plastic spit bowl.

"Good one!" I applaud her. We've begun praising her
for spitting. She's had some respiratory issues and
ridding her lungs of fluid is important. We applaud her
for pooping, too, which is also very important. *Have you
pooped today?* Just like Joy's dad's hat. It's the same sort
of question posed, for different reasons, by my son and
his wife to Peyton, now two and a half and in the midst
of potty training. "Do you have to poop?" And, not
unlike Peyton, who gets one M&M for peeing and *two*
for pooping in the big boy potty, Christina gets *mint*
M&Ms, and she can have as many as she wants, whenever she wants them.

One advantage to aging: no parents in charge of the
chocolate. Or the ice cream.

The next day, I bump into Gary on the bridge. He's on
his way into Puerto Vallarta for supplies. I'm returning
to Casa la Ventana from the *tienda* holding a bag of fresh
produce: avocados, bananas, pineapple, and tomatoes.
Bigger and beefier than Leo, Gary looks like the former
football player he is. He uses a cane, a result of bad
knees from injuries.

"Gary! Good to see you." I put down my bags and
give him a hug.

Gary and his wife, MaryAnn, escape the brutal
winter weather of the American heartland annually. In
the early years of Casa la Ventana, when Christina had
just opened her Bed & Breakfast, Gary and MaryAnn
stayed there for several weeks each winter. Rotary

members, they've been very involved in some of Christina's Boca-related charitable endeavors: the water purification program, the *Becas* scholarship program, and the clinic. I remember my first winter in Boca, when I rented the place next door to Christina. Gary and I would wave to each other each morning. He liked to sit on his patio with his morning coffee and watch me do tai chi. I can't say I enjoyed being watched, but really, he had no other option as his balcony sat directly across from mine, separated by maybe thirty yards or so, and tai chi was an important part of my recovery. I wasn't going to stop doing it every morning simply because I had an audience.

"How are you? How are those knees, Gary?"

"Great. I had 'em replaced. I'm walking pain free for the first time in years." Gary smiles. "I'm still slow, though. How are yours?"

"Good. Won't be playing tennis again anytime soon, but I can walk and I can make it up Christina's damn stairs." We both chuckle at that. He knows about those stairs.

"When did you get here?"

"Last week. I'm here for three weeks."

Gary pauses. "How's she doing?"

"Not good, Gary. She's in a lot of pain. The doctor gave her a nerve block. He ran an IV drip, a pain killer, into the worst of the tumors, the one at the base of her spine, close to the new year. So, that's helped."

"Is there anything I can do? I want to stop by, but I don't want to intrude."

"Yeah. I get it. Call first, or text. It's best to reach out to Joy. I'm sure she'd love to see you. It's just that she tires easily and has a hard time telling people it's time for them to leave."

"Does she need anything?" Gary, like me, wants only

to help. The problem is, there's little anyone except Joy can do that helps in any substantive way.

"Tell you what, she's been grooving on ice cream lately. You could bring her some ice cream. She'd love that."

"Great! Any particular flavor? What does she like?" Gary wants a sense of purpose, too.

"I know she likes lemon, and coconut, beyond that I'm not sure, but as I said, any ice cream would be appreciated. Small things like that are the things that matter to her now. Things like Joy rubbing lotion on her legs. Or a small bowl of ice cream when she wants one."

"Perfect." Gary is beaming. He has something to do and a way to contribute.

When we part ways, I begin to realize how exhausting it must be for Christina to have so many people wanting to help, to make a difference, to relieve her pain, in any way possible, no matter how small or seemingly insignificant. But all the questions require effort in order to narrow a response down to a to-do item. *Can I do anything for you? Um, no. I'm fucking dying here.* It's hard.

I'm discovering it's best not to ask, but rather wait to be asked. It takes less energy from both people. Dying people *will* tell you what they want when they want you to know.

∾

It is now Wednesday. I have not had my laptop since Friday. And I've not heard a peep from Israel.

Withdrawal has begun in earnest.

It wouldn't bother me so much, this unplugging—I'm sure it's quite healthy for me—but I have noticed how desperately I've struggled to try and recreate my laptop experience on my phone. It doesn't work. I don't like it. The screen is too small, and I hate writing on it. I want the feel of the keyboard beneath my fingertips, all ten of them, so I can keep up with my thoughts. I cannot do that with two goddamn thumbs! And autocorrect, what a scourge! I mean, really, how on earth can one communicate cogently with Big Brother interpreting what he thinks I mean?

19

UNMOORED ONCE MORE

For the past week, I've read to her from *Many Lives, Many Masters*. Some days she says *yes* when I ask if she wants me to read to her, other times she says, *maybe later*. On those days, maybe later doesn't come. I'm learning that *maybe later* means no. She says it increasingly.

We have made it about forty-five pages into the book thus far. It is the true story of a highly regarded psychiatrist's therapeutic journey with a patient wracked with phobias—for example, an extreme fear of water—recounted through their transcribed sessions. In an attempt to identify the source of the patient's fears, Dr. Weiss resorts to hypnosis. While under hypnosis, the patient suddenly begins describing a previous lifetime; in this case, a sailor who had drowned at sea. When she came out from hypnosis, she had no memory of what she had said, but her fear of water had disappeared.

This notion of reincarnation and previous lifetimes was one the doctor had never considered. He thought his patient had imagined it. But it happened over and over, through many sessions, and one by one her other phobias began to disappear as well. He was perplexed. Finally, during one session, her voice altered completely, and what Dr. Weiss called *the Masters* began communicating to him through her. They shared their wisdom about death and life, as well as intimate details about his life — like the death of his days-old son many years prior, something this patient nor any of the staff knew about. These interactions changed Dr. Weiss forever. After years of reluctance, he finally published the transcriptions and his own thoughts about the impact of this event on his life. Reading his book changed me. It gave me a hook on which to hang otherwise inexplicable aspects of human existence as well as some of my own experiences.

I had forgotten that I'd given Christina a copy years ago. When I first opened it to begin reading, I was surprised to see my inscription to her. I'm glad I did that, inscribed it. *To an old soul, with much love, from another old soul.* For four separate days I've read to her. The first time, I noticed how intently she watched me, her body curled on her left side, head turned toward me, hands tucked under the pillow beneath her head, her eyes on my face. In hindsight, I now wonder if she wasn't watching me then, soaking in the details, in the same way I observe her now, trying to memorize the minutia of her essence. But she can only take so much listening for so long, so it's basically one chapter per sitting, if that.

Today, she lays on her back, propped up on her three pillows, looking over her toes out her veranda doors to the mountains beyond the river. I've been reading maybe five minutes when suddenly, in the middle of a sentence, she stops me.

"I've had enough."

I look up from the book to her face, my eyebrows raised.

"Okay," I say. "We can pick up here tomorrow if you're up to it."

She closes her eyes. "No," she says. "I'm done with the book." And then, "Thanks for reading." And finally, "I think I'll nap now."

I feel as though I've been slapped. I sit there a minute, suddenly unmoored. I have no role again. Just like that, she has untied my little boat from the dock and shoved me out into open water once again. I get up to leave.

"Close the door," she says.

"Sure."

"Thanks." Her voice fades. She's in pain.

So am I.

"See you later."

"Yeah," she sighs. "Maybe later."

I have this horrible tendency, an emotionally driven behavioral response, that I *really* hate. I identified it years ago, and like all patterns of protection, it reappears, unbidden, in odd moments when I'm unsure, or under pressure, or, as in the current situation, without an obvious role. Well, I have a bunch of patterns like that (oh, don't we all, she says hopefully) but this one I find particularly distasteful. I don't just want to be *special*, I want to be the *most* special. I want to be the brightest and best in the room all the time. *Fuck me*. Excuse me while I puke.

And here's the thing: I only want to feel *most* special when I forget I already *am*. It's another goddamn paradox. Most of the time I feel blessed and as special as anyone else, no matter who they are, no matter my personal circumstances. I'm essentially an optimist, but life has tempered my outlook with practicalities.

It's another lens on life I find helpful, that I am both the most important and least important person in the room, simultaneously. Even Oprah comes with her crap. Fame and fortune have nothing to do with importance or value. Everyone is valuable. I truly believe that, but apparently, sometimes it seems easier to believe that about *other* people over myself. This particular pattern hadn't reared its ugly head in many years, and I had fooled myself into thinking it was not only dormant but had, in fact, disappeared. I believed it had checked out, had packed its bags and left.

I was wrong.

Watching Christina and Joy and Toto and Isabel do their daily dance of intimacy, seeing their ease of move-ment, I feel like a flimsy flip-flop in a room full of fancy flats, out of place, and less than. Intellectually, I under-stand that's a pile of hogwash, but emotionally, appar-ently, not so much. Based on results—and upon reflection—I realize that much of the standard by which I seem to measure specialness is dependent on a) having a clearly defined role and associated tasks, and b) accom-plishing those tasks successfully and on time by actually *doing* something. I feel like I've accomplished nothing, *done* nothing while here except to sit and watch Christina. And read to her. And now that's no longer happening. I try to help Joy, but often feel underfoot, a hinderance.

It's not that I need anyone to notice or acknowledge me in order to generate the feeling of being special. It's nice, of course, but not needed. I get a real kick out of the whole random acts of kindness thing and the notion of anonymous gifts. Rather, it now seems to me, the undercurrent of restlessness has more to do with me *choosing* a role—any role, whether being or doing—and acting from that.

If I had my laptop, it would be so easy to assuage the discomfort. I could at least fool myself into a false sense of accomplishment by writing something, *any*thing. I could feel special that way, you see. But even that veneer has been stripped away and I am left to examine the raw wood beneath. How do I define *special* and *valuable* and *contribution*? Where does *worth* reside? I preach the value of *being* and not focusing on doing all the damn time, yet here I go again, measuring my personal value based on my productivity, by keeping score, by comparing.

Joy tells me it is a huge help simply to be here, to give her a break from care tending. And there is value in that, I agree. My heart, however, wags a finger at me. Pushing back from the table of doing to save room for a little being is still a struggle for me.

Mary comes to mind.

It used to piss me off when they would read that passage from the New Testament in church on Sundays. The one where Mary sits at Jesus' feet, adoringly, while Jesus waxes eloquently, and she's all like, *Oh, Jesus, you say the most amazing things.* Meanwhile, while Mary lounges around, her sister, Martha, is in the kitchen making sure everybody gets fed. Martha's busy doing all the grunt work. Martha becomes upset, rather under-standably, I remember thinking as a young girl. I mean, good on Mary and all, but I remember thinking, *it's nice that Mary has Martha handling things for her.* Without Martha, Mary would have had to actually do some work. When Martha finally complains to Jesus and asks for a little help, for heaven's sake, Jesus tells her that Mary has chosen *the better part*. The better part? What the fuck does *that* mean?

I have a sinking suspicion he meant *being* versus *doing*.

And probably something about how we measure our value and where we direct our attention.

Being versus doing. *Fuck.* I've got the perfect practice ground. *Damn.* I hate practicing things I don't like and find difficult, like the dreaded F chord on the guitar I'm attempting to learn how to play.

Hmm . . . maybe it's still difficult because I haven't practiced enough to make it easy yet.

There is still no word from Israel on the status of my laptop. I am beginning to think I have made a poor choice by handing my baby over to a stranger, a handsome one, and a father to three cute kids, but a stranger, nonetheless. We connected on WhatsApp the night he made the house call. I know he's received my text asking for a status report. I can only surmise he either a) hasn't gotten the required part, or b) hasn't gotten around to repairing it yet, or c) is fucking with me, or d) has absconded to the Caymans.

How hard is it to text me back with, "I'm not done yet, but you are my top priority today, and I will get you your baby back soon!"

I'd settle for a *not done yet* response.

Some part of me suspects this whole laptop thing is a test. A fucking test on patience, or being present, or letting go, or whatever the hell it is that I didn't sign up for!

I am literally beginning to think I am addicted to my laptop. Well, not the thing itself, but what it affords me, the illusion of connection. Feeling connected to current events, or friends, or colleagues. Feeling connected to some sort of purpose, to a sense of accomplishment. Feeling connected to my body, my fingers, my mind. I've tried recording some observations, talking into that stupid smartphone, which is a poor substitute at best. It's not the same, saying the words out loud rather than writing them, seeing them emerge in print before me, my thoughts coming to life, taking form in front of my face. And then, the joy of refining them, and the experience of precision.

Creating clarity from chaos, this is what writing offers me, the sorting through as important as the end result, the process as crucial as the product. And, in this moment, without my laptop, without my coping mechanisms and machines, I am left to look at the symptoms of withdrawal and the lessons to be learned from confronting them head-on.

They say life is a school and you get your degree when you die. I'm not ready to die. I'm not even that sad. But I am scared. I'm scared of losing Christina. I'm scared of these feelings of unrest in my belly, indicators of lessons yet to be absorbed.

And, at the moment, I'm weary of school.

20

BROKEN BITS OF BEAUTY

Joy sits on the single portico step at the top of the stairs. She's got her head lowered and a pen in her hand. She is making a list and smoking a cigarette.

"Hey," I say walking up the brick stairway from my room below. "What's happening?"

"The queen has a task for us." Joy cocks her head to one side, towards four clear plastic bags filled with seashells, small rocks, and broken bits of brightly colored tiles. "She wants us to place them around the gardens."

"Okay." I pick up one bag and examine it. There are a lot of pieces in each bag. This is not a thirty-minute task. "This will take a while. How come? I mean, what *are* these?"

Joy takes a drag of her cigarette—one of her allotted five for the day—lifts her eyebrows and tilts her head in a quick, brief movement. She smiles as she exhales and gives a loving eye-roll.

"It's stuff she's collected from old projects, from when they built. Old bits and pieces. She found them when we cleaned out her bathroom. You know, that storage space under the staircase on her side." Joy returns to her list.

The storage area on the other side of Christina's bedroom awaits a thorough cleansing. The big one with all the books in the lending library, and the cleaning supplies, and extra household necessities like toilet paper and soap and shampoo. Cleaning that out is next on Christina's list. Alesia is here to help Joy carry out that day-long task.

Joy gets up to stub out her smoke in the ceramic ashtray on the small wrought iron table a few feet away. It has become my outside desk of sorts, my phone, pad and pens sit atop it. She points to the large terracotta flowerpots that line the portico entrance. There are four knee-high planters filled with prayer lilies as tall as your waist.

"I've started. I figure if we do a little each day we'll eventually get them all distributed. Somewhere." She shoots me an impish grin. "She'll never know where they end up. Hell, she won't even be coming out the front door anymore."

Humor: an antidote to pain.

There must be over fifty potted plants in the garden, all shapes and sizes, all over the place, tucked into rock curvatures, balanced on walls, hanging from tree branches. I walk to the pots Joy has indicated and look. Joy has created a mini mosaic in a circular pattern around the base of the plant utilizing shells, stones, *and* tiles. It's quite lovely, obviously something any passerby would stop, notice, and admire. *Here lives someone who cares about plants.* My thoughts on random placement of Christina's remnants, of tossing them hither and yon, quickly skip away. I must be attentive to this process, I realize, regardless of whether or not Christina will ever see the result of my efforts.

The word *reverence* bubbles in my brain. If she thought enough about these broken bits to bother collecting them, and then to bother asking that they adorn her beloved gardens, then I can be reverent about my fulfillment of her request. Besides, seeing what Joy produced twigged my creativity button.

Oh, okay, it also twigged my competition button.

Oh, goody. An opportunity to practice not caring about not being the most special.

Joy is off to Puerto Vallarta with Leo and the list. She leaves me in charge, reminding me to feed the animals if they're not back by 5:00 p.m. As if I need a reminder. The animals will remind me themselves.

Isabel has left for the day. Luisa, the manicurist, has come and gone, too, leaving Christina's fingernails freshly polished. Once Christina was no longer able to leave Casa la Ventana, Luisa began coming to Boca by bus in order to continue to tend to Christina's hands and feet. Such is the level of devotion Christina elicits.

Christina is napping. The house is quiet. I sit in the garden outside the front portico, at the small metal table and its four matching chairs. With the exception of a couple of hours in the afternoon when the light plays on the ground, chasing itself through the palm fronds high above, the garden is in complete shade and offers a respite from the humidity and sun drenched heat.

I sit there, in silence, without anything to do. I have nothing to do, that is, except to ward off any unwanted visitors. There has been an increasing stream of people who just want to stop by and chat, but Christina no longer has the energy—a polite way of saying *tolerance*—for anything unexpected. People with appointments, those she's invited and is expecting at a certain time, she will tell the household to allow in. If you're not on the list, you will be turned away. *Maybe later.* But even an appointment is no guarantee. If Christina suddenly tires, the plans are dissolved and delayed until another day. I've had to turn several people away.

I hear the sounds of tiny feet coming up the brick staircase. Bella barks once from inside, and then silence; whoever is headed up is known to her. The little girls are back. Maybe seven and five years of age, they want to see Christina. Again. They have stopped by twice already this week. People have become accustomed to wandering in during the day; Casa la Ventana's front door usually stands wide open.

They ask if Christina is here. That much I can understand. I mime that Christina is sleeping. Again. I can see the disappointment in their eyes. What they really want is to swim in the pool. It is the reason they have climbed so many steps. Swimming in the pool is a delicious delight Christina used to allow *los niños* on Sundays. But it's not Sunday. This is the third time this week they've trotted up the stairs with hopeful hearts spread open in their warm, chocolate brown eyes. They are barefoot and their hair is unkempt. The older girl does the talking. I hitch up my shoulders and murmur *mas tardes* a couple of times. Then, *mañana*.

"Ella no esta bien. Ella esta enferma," I explain.

"Si." They already know, but they are fond of her and the pool—all the children are—and miss both. I smile a lot and look sympathetic to their plight. I'm good at that, looking like I'm sympathetic to the person's request as I deny it. I say *no* much better now than I did even a decade ago. When you dance with death, you get selfish with your choices.

The girls retreat down the stairs. They'll be back. I return to my seat at the table, noticing the pattern of the bricks of the patio beneath my bare feet and the cement that holds them in place.

I'm like that cement, I think. Not the *bricks* themselves—the caretaking, the list making, the direction giving—but rather a part of the substance between, that which holds the bricks together. For four Fridays and the days between, I am here to lend safety, security, and stability to Christina's daily existence. By *being* here, being here by the door, shepherding, or maybe sheepdogging. I separate the herd.

And suddenly I know my role. I know my purpose! I know by the relief that floods my body and the sigh my soul makes in the recognition of it. I am the Guardian At The Gate. *Her* gate, at least. No light swords or rabid dogs accompany my post at this table, but no one can get by me. I may not be as permanent as the cement, but I'm as powerful. The paradox that this role requires little beyond simply sitting—no doing, per se, only being—is not lost on me. That, plus the fact that I have no laptop, no immediately available way to feel productive while manning my post.

The Universe says, *Just sit there and guard the door, dearie. Don't do, just be.*

I feel a bit chastised, as though I should have already known better. The realization feels akin to moments in my childhood when my father would call me from my bedroom using my full name. "Cynthia Mary, you come down here right now, young lady!" he would bellow up the staircase, and I knew I was in trouble. This moment is sort of like that, but a whole lot gentler.

Wait. What? Holy smokes! My middle name is *Mary*. No, for real, it's Mary! I dropped it when I married the first time and inserted my maiden name, Cook, as my middle name.

Hmm . . . maybe there's a message here . . . ?

21

DEATH DURING LIFE

The tumors are growing.

The ones along her spine are expanding their reach, their tendrils seeking new prey to poison. She has new tumors appearing on her head now, too. I catch her in moments unaware, her eyes glazed, looking through the open double doors of the veranda out to her precious mountains to the east.

Her right hand moves to her head where her fingertips seek to measure the masses growing on her skull. They vary in size. They are not lumps so much as they are slightly raised portions of her head made noticeable only through touch. She rolls onto her right side one day. Her left hand creeps up and behind her back and comes to rest at the base of her spine. She begins massaging the area. I watch her from the large leather recliner to the left of her bed, four feet from the door. It's not only comfortable, it rocks, too, which I find soothing.

She has turned away from me, toward the eastern veranda where the majestic mango tree drips its lush greenness over the side of the balcony railing. Beyond it rises the tail end of the Sierra Madres. And, at the very

top of one peak, out of place amongst the other vegeta-
tion at that height, grows a singular palm tree, dubbed,
Palma Sola. It is her favorite thing upon which to gaze.
Something about its lofty, solitary silhouette and majestic
defiance of the odds speaks to her. She wants her ashes
buried beneath it.

"It's the view I'll miss most," she had said to me one
day back in May. "The mountains." She had given her
head a slight shake and turned to face me. "That might
sound weird. I should miss the people, I suppose. But
this view . . . this place . . ." Her voice had trailed off
then, and her eyes turned back to the mountains beyond
her bedroom veranda doors. She gazes at them
constantly now.

"It's getting bigger. Here. Feel here," she instructs
me.

I get up from the recliner, surprised to be invited, and
extend my right hand. She takes it in her left and guides
me to the largest of the tumors growing at the base of her
spine. I am surprised by how hard it feels under my
fingertips. She presses my hand firmly against the mass,
moving it about. I am surprised by that, too. The pressure she applies is far more than I expected from her; her
hands are still strong.

"Doesn't it hurt to press like that?" I ask.

"No, that's the one where they put the nerve block. In
the middle there, I don't feel anything." She pauses, then
adds, "At least, not right now."

The week before Christmas the pain had been so
intense, so debilitating, that Joy was afraid Christina
wouldn't make it to the 25th. Joy was up a couple of
nights with her, tending to her. Christina reported that
the pain was a ten out of ten on the pain scale, mostly
emanating from the largest tumor affixed to her coccyx.
This made any form of movement excruciating, even

sitting. Finally, the doctor came and inserted an IV nerve
block agent of some sort, greatly relieving her pain. By
the time I arrived on January 4th she had rebounded to
the point that her pain level was only a two or three for
the first ten days or so of my visit.

But the large tumor has continued to grow since the
nerve block, and its new tendrils are not deadened. No,
those new nerve endings are very much alive and her
days are a race against their invasive pain. If she can
keep it at under a five, she can function, she says. So,
that's the game, to keep the pain below a five. It's a race,
and one she can't win, and she knows that, but in the
short term, it's a purpose that fuels her higher one, to
leave this plane, this place and these people, feeling
complete.

"I still have shit to do," she says.

Later, we talk about the end and her options. She
mentions fentanyl patches. She had used them for a week
before Christmas, before the nerve block. "I still have
two. Ten would do it."

"What? Would do what?"

"Take me out." She has thought about this, ending it
herself, if the pain gets unbearable. I suppose that's
normal, but I find it disconcerting to hear her say it out
loud, as jarring as an off-key note in the middle of a song.

"I could get more. There are people who can get them
for me." Christina knows somebody for everything.

"What, you'd just plaster yourself with them?"

"Uh huh. Overdose." Christina looks out her veranda
doors again. "I'd just go to sleep and not wake up. Joy
could peel them off afterwards. Nobody would know."
Silence. Then, "If it gets as bad as it was . . ." She leaves
the thought hanging. We both know it will get that bad
again, eventually.

"Can you get another block?" I ask, desperate to

avoid the thought of her in so much pain that she'd choose to exit this world on her own.

"No. They can only do it once." More silence. Then, "Maybe it won't come to that. Maybe I'll go peacefully in my sleep." She feigns a small smile indicating she doubts it. She reaches out and scratches behind Bella's ear, strokes her head. "Right, Miss Bella? Fall asleep and not wake up again. A good way to go." Her head falls back onto her pillow. She is suddenly tired. Thoughts of future pain and a possible exit strategy have worn her out.

"But not yet," she says as her eyes close. "I still have shit to do."

Christina is an avid reader with myriad books on indigenous flora and fauna, and her garden is alive and lush with all kinds of floral delights: palm trees, fruit trees, flowering trees. She has a first-class green thumb and can make anything grow—plants *and* people—and her garden reflects that gift. She spent years creating it, planting and tending and cultivating and moving things around, and adding to it, always adding to it. Every trip to town, she'd return with another planter or green growth of some kind. She is particularly fond of her orchids, and all sorts of vivid varieties poke out from tree crooks or hang from branches in a portion of the garden near the front portico. She has dubbed it Gramma's Garden.

There are dozens of potted plants and flowers—on the ground, in hanging baskets, affixed to trees. Birds of paradise. Bougainvillea in white, yellow, orange and fuchsia. Hibiscus plants with blooms eight-inches wide. Christmas plants and waist-high peace lilies. Verdant and varied, Christina's garden holds hidden beauty if you simply stop, stand still, and look around.

In the middle of the main portion of the garden there is an old tree. Its trunk is at least fifteen inches in diameter. It may not be as aged as its nearby neighbor a few feet away, but it is a tree Christina left standing and intentionally built around. There were many other large, older trees she insisted on saving. This particular tree, however, unlike its nearby cousins, is no longer healthy and thriving. It has been consumed by an invasive parasitic plant. That sounds ugly, as though the tree would appear withered and decrepit itself, but it's not. Though dead with its top lopped off, the trunk of the tree is tall and straight and covered from top to bottom with a crawling ivy-like growth. It appears attractive and very much alive to the casual passing eye.

But it kills. Just like cancer, this parasitic ivy sucks the life blood from its host. Right there, in the middle of a garden resplendent in color and shape and size, a garden vital and throbbing with life, exists death. It permeates the soil, the plants, and this particular tree. There's no real reason for it. Why this tree and not its neighbor?

I remember something Christina told to me once, years ago, when I was first learning about how to deal with mildew, a seasonal reality for the locals. She told me to drag the curtains and sheets outside on my balcony, drape them over the railing, spray some Lysol over the fabric, and let them bake in the sun all day.

"Fungus grows in the dark," she said. "Sunlight kills germs."

So does awareness.

We walk around each day, every one of us, witnessing life while blind to the death that drives it, destroys it, and nourishes it at the same time. And so, in our blindness, we become blind to life, too. We grow numbed—by the news, by the unnecessary and excessive, by the cultural norms for success and what it should look like—and thereby numb ourselves to the very essence of life for which we yearn: peace.

Until we know our expiration date. And then? Everything changes. Like going from greyscale back to color, the mundane becomes meaningful, and petty perishes in the wake of gratitude.

We humans flail frantically in pursuit of a faux fantasy, the promise of a pain-free life. But it doesn't exist—because we're human.

Dammit.

∾

Mary Oliver, the Pulitzer prize winning poet, died of lymphoma last night. She was eighty-three years old, ahead of her time, and straddled the space between words and feelings, and between life and death. She was in the world but not of it.

I have admired her writing for decades. The first time I read her poem, *Wild Geese*, it reduced me to tears. My throat still clenches each time I read it. Her words reek of wisdom won on the battlefield of life. Her death, the current loss of my laptop, and the impending loss of Christina form an ugly, telling trifecta. I am surrounded by death, disease, and separations.

The euphemistic acronym GIGO comes to mind, a relic from the early days of the computer age: garbage in, garbage out. It's the same with our attention. Whether it be performing our daily personal and professional tasks or planning and preparing for some significant event or milestone, the quality of attention paid during the process itself can determine the level of fulfillment derived from its result.

I remember something Alan told me toward the end of his life. "I am *very* careful about where I direct my attention," he said. "My energy follows, and it's limited. I have no energy for anything other than that which uplifts and inspires and renews me. If it doesn't bring me joy, I've got no time for it."

Energy in, energy out. Thank you, Alan.

Whether mundane or mighty, do I give the same quality of attention to all things I do/think/say each day? As though all things are equal? As though all people are important? Where do I direct my attention, and why? These are emerging as significant questions for me to consider while I watch Christina direct her diminishing energy toward areas that, at least in her mind, still require her attention.

So, I sit in Christina's garden and gaze at the beautiful expressions of nature's abundant variety. Life blooms before me in a garden tended with love, while death inches behind me, in a bedroom built with foresight. More paradoxes. I'm beginning to believe that finding a balance within them, an internal accounting and reconciliation, may be required of us all before we can possibly find peace, before we, like Mary Oliver's geese, are able to *find our place in the family of things*.

Oh, dear. She was a Mary, *too!*

Uh, oh.

22

LINES LAID

Don stops by unannounced, again.

He continues to do so even after reprimands and dismissals. There is always a reason why: his phone died, the internet was out, her line was busy. It is an increasing source of anxiety for Christina, wondering when he'll pop in and how long he'll stay. Don tends to become agitated easily. She sometimes has difficulty getting him to leave.

He sits in the leather lounger. On my way down the stairs from the kitchen above, as I pass by Christina's room, I pop my head around the corner of her doorjamb in such a way that my face is obscured from Don's view. I catch her eye.

"All good?" I whisper, raising my eyebrows and tilting my head. "Do you need anything?" She knows I'm really asking, "Do you want me to stay?"

"Oh, hey," she says with a full voice. "Yeah, I'm good. Don stopped by. We're discussing his next move." That's my invitation to join them. She's become formal, even toned, removed; her guard is up.

I turn toward Don, lean against the doorjamb, all

casual interest. He can't see that I've also grabbed an invisible scalpel. In case. "Yeah? Where're you heading, Don?"

"The marina, I think. They have a couple of nice units up for rent. I'm going to see them next week."

"Why are you moving?"

Don's mouth sours and he waves his hand in a dismissive motion. "My place is crap. I can't get the internet working and there's no phone signal. And it's too dark. I don't get any sun until late afternoon—"

Christina interrupts him. "I reminded Don that the internet company will send out a service man and get his internet working properly. And a landline phone would solve his cell issues." Don waves her words away. It's obvious that Don's list was in fact much longer, and he would have enjoyed continuing to share his lengthy complaints had she not stopped him. Christina is using her mommy voice. She is also handing the baton over to me.

"Hang on. Let me join you." I grab a small wooden desk chair from the foyer area—a child's chair, really—and drag it into the bedroom past Don's feet to the foot of the bed facing Christina. I join the conversation, which, at each and every turn, returns to some complaint.

A few weeks before I visited her in May, Christina moved Don into an apartment, but he found endless reasons to return to Casa la Ventana. He hates his new apartment, he says, but I suspect he'd hate any apartment. For the price, it's a great place, actually. I'd live there. It sits atop a sheer cliff overlooking the Pacific Ocean. Don can see the stunning sunsets every evening, something blocked from our side of the river in Boca, and I remark how lucky he is to have that view.

"Seen one, you've seen 'em all," he responds with a wave of his hand. Dismissed.

Don dismisses a lot of things these days. His slow-moving dementia has reduced his thought patterns from linear to circular. He feels cheated by life. He is confused and angry, and, unfortunately, sees Christina as the source of many (if not all) of his growing limitations and associated anxiety. Inevitably, their conversations devolve into disagreements. For years, Christina has tried to help Don manage his finances and medical appointments. He stubbornly refuses to accept input, assistance, or clarification. Don feels safer in the past. That doesn't make him a bad guy, on the contrary, he can be warm and amiable when he wants. But he's a rudderless ship now, without purpose or direction, fueled by blame and victimhood.

Willful ignorance spares people the pain of accountability.

Christina is quiet, watching me take the lead and say the things I know she appreciates me expressing on her behalf. After a while, friends can read each other's body language and minuscule facial movements, things others might miss or misinterpret. I'm upbeat and engaged with Don, turning his attention from Christina, who is on his right, to me on his left. This protects Christina from his view. I see her head lop back onto the pillows. Listening to Don tires her.

It's been a journey of letting go for her. Christina has her own control issues, as does Joy, and myself, if I'm honest. Birds of a feather. But the journey of releasing Don to his own devices, knowing his diagnosis—and now hers—has been particularly intense for her, fraught with ethical and moral implications, not to mention the physical and emotional impact of her answers.

I asked her by phone months prior, "Do you think he gets it? That you're dying?"

"No. I beat it before; he thinks I'll beat it again. He cannot grasp that there is no cure this time or that I'm choosing no treatment," she said. "He won't get it until I die."

Here's what I think. Christina has a right to whatever the hell she wants at this point with no questions asked. She wants a BLT she gets a BLT. She wants more lotion on her feet, she gets more lotion. She wants ice cream, the only response is "What kind?" She wants Don gone, he's gone. Period. Done. Next.

Listening to Don now, in person, and watching him while he speaks, instead of hearing Christina recount their conversations, I better understand some of her past frustrations. It's subtle but apparent. Don is incapable of consistent coherent thought, with only circular reasoning on display. Additional visual data floods my trained eye. His face reflects information he is unaware he's communicating. He smiles at inappropriate moments, breaks eye contact at telling points when answering a question, or becomes briefly enraged at the smallest provocation, his nostrils flaring and eyes narrowing in microscopic flashes which reveal his internal truth.

Somewhere in the middle of the twenty-minute visit, absorbing Christina's grateful energy for my presence and sensing the soothing I seem to provide Don, I realize that *this* is also something I can do, a role I can play, that of facilitator. I can guard a door and act as mediator, go-between. And I'm better at *that* than I am at cooking bacon. I can be an interface between them. She has not the heart to deny him access completely—she is too kind at her core—but she must draw boundaries with him to protect the short time she has left, as well as prepare him for the time ahead without her.

"So, Don. Where are you off to? Lunch on the beach?" I say, attempting to close the conversation. I sit up straighter, put my hands on my thighs, and straighten my shoulders. Subtle signals. *Time to go.*

Don doesn't move.

Christina raises her head from the pillows, taking my cue. "Yeah, I need to rest, Don. I need to limit visit lengths, too, these days. Ten minutes. Takes too much out of me."

Don continues to look at her without moving. "Oh, okay. Yeah. Sure."

I rise from my tiny chair at the foot of the bed. Momma bear is standing and is fearsome. Beware the scalpel. I hold out my right hand. "Come on, Don. I'll walk you out."

Don doesn't move. He looks back to Christina, unused to the apparent shift in authority. "So, when can I come back?"

"I don't know, Don. Email me," Christina responds. She's tired.

"I have. But you don't answer." Don is dangerously close to complaining again.

"That means no, then. It means I haven't seen it yet or am sleeping or am in too much pain, Don." Christina sinks further into the pillows. "But no response does not mean yes. You just can't stop by, Don. Not anymore. You need to check with me first. Okay? Call me instead of email."

"Okay." Don is too quick to respond, and his voice is too chipper.

"No, Don, I need you to hear me. I mean it." Christina uses the word *need* a lot these days.

Don feels called out. He pushes back. "I don't see why I need to ask permission to visit my own home, the one I helped build. You seem to have forgotten that." He has become a truculent teenager.

Christina sighs from the pillows. "I haven't forgotten. We've already discussed this, *all* of this." She closes her eyes again. I jump in.

"Tell you what, Don, you agree to *call* before stopping by, and we'll leave the internet out of it. It's easier for you. Call the day before and see how she's feeling. Is that good with you?"

Don turns his attention to me, noticing my outstretched hand as though for the first time. He takes it and stands before saying, "Okay. Call before coming. Will do."

I walk him out and listen to him for another few minutes—all things I'd already heard him say—before finally hugging him goodbye. The scalpel has been sheathed. I may be a momma bear, but I have compassion for my prey.

Christina turns her head toward me when I come back. "Thank you. Do me a favor. Lock the door." I scurry over the smooth, terracotta tiles of the foyer just beyond her bedroom, flip the dead bolt on the front door, and return.

"Done."

"Thanks. I don't want him coming back. He'll forget some little thing and use it as pretext for returning. He exhausts me. And thanks for the help with boundaries. He doesn't get it. You running interference while you're here will help."

She closes her eyes and sighs deeply. She's doing that more often, too, sighing. "I think we better start locking the door every time we go in or out." She opens her eyes and gives me a faint smile. "Well, anytime *you* guys go in or out." She pauses. "I need to tell Joy. And Toto and Isabel." More needs.

"Speaking of needs, you want some lunch?" I ask. Joy's downstairs doing laundry and I'm on watch.

"Thanks, no. Not hungry." Her sentences are shortening. "Need a nap. Would you get me an edible? One is enough."

"Sure. What flavor?" I move to her vanity and open the plastic container holding all the medications.

"I don't care."

I grab a watermelon gummy. "Anything else? When was your last pain pill? You want an Advil?" I realize that's too many questions for her right now as soon as they shoot from my mouth.

"No. Just sleep."

"Okay." I hand her the gummy and she chews it slowly while I stand and watch at her bedside, at the ready with water bottle in hand. "Maybe I'll head down to the pool." It's a beautiful sunny day after a few cloudy ones.

"Go." She's looking out the French doors in front of her, not at me. "I would if I were you." She finishes the gummy, takes a sip from the water bottle, hands it back to me, and then gently settles back into a sleeping position. Her eyes close. "Lock the door behind you when you go."

"Will do." I lean down and kiss her forehead before leaving. "See you later."

"Yeah," she says with little enthusiasm, "maybe later." Her eyes stay shut. The pain is back, and Don's visit has siphoned her reserves for the day. She's done. I doubt I will see her again today and for a brief moment am angry at Don for stealing time that somehow feels as though it should have been mine.

In the midst of that flash I suddenly feel for Don. Imagine his anger and confusion.

Maybe later.

23

THE GREAT PURGE

I climb the outside stairs from my bedroom—dubbed El Rio—to the front door. I'm heading to the kitchen to refill my coffee cup, but right away I can tell something is up. The front door stands wide open and there is a burgeoning collection of stuff covering the floor of the portico. Old stuff. Bags of stuff. Stuff covered in dust: old mops, buckets, rags, rugs, pictures, and books. Rounding the corner of the staircase, empty mug in hand, I see that the clutter continues throughout the area called the foyer, though it is the size of a large bedroom. The space is really Christina's office area, such as it is these days: a desk, a chair, a printer, and a tall wooden filing cabinet. She had the desk made by a local artisan, something she does as often as is possible as long as it's practical and within budget. Christina is nothing if not practical and prudent. But she is also generous and has supported many local artists.

The desktop is piled with manila folders and the detritus of Casa la Ventana's daily life: scattered pens and pencils, a stack of copy paper, Maya's medicine and dropper, a hair clip, half a slice of dried toast on a napkin. A large wood cabinet sits against the opposite wall across from her desk. It holds sheets and towels used for Bed & Breakfast guests. Over the years, its storage cubbies have become unruly, with their contents shoved in where they'll fit rather than in an organized, neat fashion. Joy intends to correct that effrontery.

It is the day of the great purge, the day the foyer and its large adjoining storage area under the main stairway are to be cleaned and weaned. Joy has already begun, pulling things off the shelves and out of the closet, sorting the stuff it contains into various groupings, hence the floor clutter. There are bags of new bed pillows, still in their plastic covers, then stuffed inside larger green trash bags—Christina's method of waging war on moisture and mildew in a humid climate—and then finally edged into indentations under the stairs. There are bags of towels, brand new, and sheet sets, and bedspreads, and bathmats, and all kinds of replacement parts for the engine of a finely tuned B&B. Most of the dust-covered green trash bags, though, are unmarked and must be opened and examined before sorting, something Joy will ensure is *not* the case the next time someone tries to clean out this particular area. She sighs and clucks her tongue in rhythm to her discoveries.

"When was the last time *this* was opened?"

"Oh my god! We are *so* tossing *this*!"

"I can't *believe* all this crap. And some of it's *good* crap just waiting to be found. It just needs a *place*." Joy is all about things in their proper places, the ones *she* determines.

I keep moving toward the kitchen. When I return with a full mug of hot coffee, Joy has cleared off the large desk chair to make space for Christina. "We're going to see if we can get the Queen out of her bed. She needs to make some decisions so we can finish this."

I grab the smaller chair, the child-sized desk chair, sit down, and make myself as small and still as possible. You don't mess with Joy's process unless asked. Even random-looking piles have a purpose that perhaps only she can see at the moment, but in the end, all will be made clear, so best to stay the hell out of the way when Joy's cleaning.

Joy organizes with the same sort of panache and focus as Christina cooks or I facilitate, with love, determination, precision, and focus. Joy's the kind of person who cleans with a toothbrush—something I've never done in my whole life—and she finds dirt other people never even knew existed in the first place. It's insane. She claims it's her OCD. Maybe. But I think she simply enjoys cleaning so much, the before-and-after of it, that she has become a black belt cleaning champion with a rag and spray cleaner. I'm that way with laundry; I love to fold laundry precisely, evenly, and then stack it and see the finished product. I find it distinctly satisfying. It also helps that I only do laundry for myself these days.

Joy's cleaning process, however, takes a *long* time, a much longer time than any of my laundry tasks. Christina's storage area holds a lot of stuff. The ceilings are ten feet tall. This might become a two-day endeavor. First, Joy empties the shelves inside the closet of all their crap —the cleaning supplies and paper products and light-bulbs and soap—then she drags in a stepladder and climbs it so she can wash down each shelf. Then she reloads all the stuff, in order, face front, in neat rows, like a retail store displaying its inventory. Then she moves onto the next set of shelving units.

Alesia helps. She holds the ladder. She hands things up and takes things away, out of the closet, adding to the growing piles. Back and forth she goes. I sit in my small chair and watch, sipping my coffee and feeling slightly guilty for not helping—Joy and Alesia glisten with sweat —but it's a small space, I'd get in the way and only slow things down. They've got a rhythm going. And I'm practicing my Mary shit, okay? And, besides, they're twenty-five years younger. All these reasons keep me rooted to my chair. That, plus I don't really *want* to help.

Eventually, Joy decides it's time for Christina to join us and we get her out of bed and into the large padded desk chair. Alesia flutters about making sure Christina is comfortable—a box to hold her legs up, a shawl around her shoulders—and Joy starts in.

"Okay, lady. Let's go through some things first, things I *think* I know what they are, or what they do, or where they go. Then we'll get to the questionable stuff."

Off they go, Joy holding something up, Christina explaining its purpose and placement, Joy handing whatever it is to Alesia, and Alesia putting it somewhere. Along the way some things are placed back in the storage area under the stairs. They are put away in their *proper places*, according to Joy, the places that *make sense*. The larger piles start to shift; some diminish while others grow. The give-it-away and trash piles are the largest.

When Joy moves the ladder to the bookshelves, I get off my chair and offer to help with the unloading, thinking more hands will make for fewer trips to the foyer where we can sort through them, which was an entirely logical assumption, I thought.

Joy did not. "I'm not ready for that yet."

Chastened, I slink back to my chair. I can tell that Christina is beginning to tire of the questions and the talking, as well as the time and attention this project requires. Joy is tiring of the time and effort, too; she's the one sweating, and she wants this off her to-do list. Alesia just wants to help, and I want to stay out of the way. I'm doing a mean impression of Mary, and rather enjoying it, to tell the truth. It seems you must practice enough the stuff that's hard to find any appreciation for it.

For the next hour, I watch a play in three acts unfold before my eyes.

Act 1: "I love you, but, goddammit, what a mess."

. . . wherein the two protagonists, the crone and the maiden, in an attempt to accomplish the grand plan, find themselves becoming indecisive and short in their replies. Decisions are delayed and delegated. The maiden is displeased. The crone becomes aggravated. The two side-kicks try to stay small and silent. Their presence is clearly extraneous.

Act 2: "Somebody else make the damn decisions."

. . . wherein the two sidekicks, feeling sidelined and useless, offer helpful suggestions, but for the most part try to stay the hell out of the way. Books are removed from the shelves. Books are returned to the shelves. It's become another walk down memory lane. Some progress made, but it's agonizingly slow.

Act 3: "Whatever. Fuck it. Back to bed."

. . . wherein the crone realizes only she can make most of the keep/get rid of decisions or answer the "What the hell is this?" questions and is wearied by the weight of the knowledge. She has lived long enough. She is tired. She hands the wand of wisdom to the maiden and wishes her good luck and farewell and takes to her bed. The maiden taps the wand, and everything is made clean and tidy. The sidekicks smile at each other and sigh with relief.

~Curtain~

Somewhere along the way, after Joy confirms that she is, indeed, ready for the books to be gone through, I have a thought to take one or two for myself. Christina tells us all to take whatever we want. The thing is, the shelves abound with what I call beach books, and none seem worth their weight or space in my suitcase to bother toting home. However, I find one paperback that looks interesting, a book about the art of conversation. Flipping to the table of contents, I decide it might be worth carting back to Toronto. Maybe I'll read it over the summer at the cottage. I put the book aside to take to my room.

Later I have another thought: I must ask Christina if I may have a pair of her earrings. There's been no indication that she's pulled something aside for me, a parting gift, a remembrance I might treasure, but perhaps that will come when I leave. In any case, I think to myself, another reason to keep the book. I'll ask Christina to inscribe it to me.

As the thought scurries across my brain in a flash — a toss-away morsel in my daily diet of chatter — I notice it. And I don't like it. Envy. Comparison. Future feeling instead of present feeling.

Note to self: Pay attention, fool. Stay *here* in the moment. Enjoy whatever it contains, with or without fucking earrings. *Geez.*

24

IN SEARCH OF PEACE

Once, about two decades ago, Christina took her son, Nate, to Las Vegas to celebrate becoming an adult when he turned twenty-one. When they got to the casino, Christina prepared Nate for his first gambling experience. She handed him a cup of quarters and then instructed him, "Now, you must *feel* the winning machine. *Feel* the floor of the casino. *Then* choose."

Christina has allowed her intuition and feelings to guide her choices all her life. She was married three times. The first was a young *blip*. The second produced her only child. The third, and longest, was to Don. Christina struggled to maintain a successful relationship and judged herself harshly for it. She never lacked for male companionship but was attracted to autonomous men who pushed back, which prevented her from gaining the sense of control she craved. Much of her journey towards peace, she tells me, is about forgiving herself for what she once perceived as failures. She wants to release fragments of regret before she goes, she says, because she wants to be at peace when she dies. She wants to feel grateful for everything at the end.

She turns her head toward me as I sit in the recliner, watching her, as I do each day now. I just sit here, just be here. She looks directly at me but says nothing for a few seconds. Then, her head slowly returns to center, and her gaze back to the mountain over her toes out the French doors in front of her. Silence. She stares out those doors more and more each day when she's awake. Joy and Isabel can be chattering away at her bedside in the morning and Christina will gaze out her doors to the mountains beyond, seemingly deaf to their voices.

"I know what it feels like," she says at last. And then, "The valley." Then, more silence.

Her head lolls back toward me. There's a sadness to the tilt of her neck, a giving way, a surrender. She looks right at me, through me.

"I am in the valley of the shadow of death," she says softly, slightly breathlessly but succinctly, as though reading a shopping mall map that states, *You are here.* This doesn't really help me, though. I am not in her mall. I assume a passive face, one I hope communicates that I'm here, I'm listening, that I understand.

Well, two out of three ain't bad, I suppose. I think that she thinks I'll understand what she's trying to communicate, that I can relate to her experience in the valley and will somehow understand where she is in it. That's what she's telling me—it's in her eyes, the intense way she's looking at me. But I *don't* know about any valley of the shadow of death! Hell, no. I may have died twice, and been revived, but I never had a shadow experience! I went rushing into death both times, headfirst, sprinting. I went from light to dark, from on to off, from life to death, in *minutes*, not months. I never saw any stinking shadow, and certainly no big-ass valley. Christina is wandering her way through it, examining the nooks and crannies and hidden places for tiny treasures.

Like plastic hitchhiking hands. But I am lost. Lost outside her mall. I have no idea where she is or what she's experiencing or what the fuck she's staring at out those stupid veranda doors or what on earth she's thinking or how I can possibly help. I keep all that to myself. I'm hoping mind-reading abilities don't accompany those who enter the valley.

You can sit a long time in silence when someone is wandering in that valley. Gives a person plenty of time to consider greys in a world that values black and white so damn much.

It's a kind of parlor conversation. "How do you want to die?" Most people answer something along the lines of *peacefully, in my sleep*. Everybody says *peacefully*. Caveats include *surrounded by my loved ones*. Some men make a joke of it. *In bed, making love to a beautiful woman.* If offered the choice between going quickly and painlessly or going by cancer, I don't know anyone who would choose the latter; the long, protracted pain; the deterioration of the body. No, we want to go quickly, without death and its relentless march to our bedside wracking us with fear and foreboding when we actually stop long enough to consider its arrival. We'll do anything to avoid pain, especially the pain of loss.

But whose pain? Is it easier on our loved ones, the ones we want surrounding us at the end, if we leave them quickly, suddenly? Painless for *us* perhaps, but not those left behind in shock and grieving. They suffer the loss. They shoulder the pain. I've always said I want to go from a heart attack, to just drop dead. But now?

My father went suddenly, thirty years ago. He was alone in the house and was found at the bottom of the basement stairs. We think it was a heart attack, though it could have been a stroke. It didn't matter. Either way, he was gone. A larger-than-life influence in the lives of his six children, he was suddenly just *gone*. It took years for us to work that crap through to completion.

Here's what I suspect while watching Christina wander through the valley: If we get to choose how we go, I'm thinking Christina's way might be a higher choice, the higher consciousness choice. Perhaps on a spiritual level, the joy of sparing those she loves the pain of incompletion — that they would feel upon her passing were it sudden — in some miraculous way offsets the pain she's bearing on a physical level. Perhaps that conscious walk toward an earmarked death lends a purpose and provides her the strength to shoulder the pain involved in a protracted exit.

I really don't want to die in some awful, painful way, but if that's the path I end up walking someday, it is comforting to know I have someone I love showing me what courage and grace and determination looks like. Because the people I leave behind will also have the opportunity to say what they want to say in order to feel complete, and that is all that matters in the long run.

Incompletion leaves a hole that is as pronounced and visible to the soul as the one a moth leaves in its wake once it flutters from its feeding ground.

Israel, my computer guru, finally responds to my texts. He's waited until Friday afternoon — my third Friday — to tell me, "They sent the wrong part." *Wha-a-t?* At this point, I just want my baby back. Broken or not, I don't care; I just want my laptop back. *Oh, no,* I think. He wouldn't like, just *keep* it, would he? This could be a ransom situation. Best to play it safe.

"That's too bad," I text back, choosing to communicate empathy. "Guess I'll need to get it fixed back home." *Solution focus.* "When do you think you'll be able to get it to me? Obviously, for your standard fee." The pleading begins. "Or maybe I can meet you . . .? But I'm thinking, please, no, don't make me find you, just bring back my baby.

I hear nothing back. The agony of separation is ebbing, and the lack of specific information in a language I can understand does little to assuage my sneaking sense that the loss of my laptop is, in fact, a mirror for the loss of Christina. And that pisses me off, because I also suspect I'll get my laptop back when I let her go. And not only do I *not* want to do that, I am not ready to do that, not yet.

Fuck you, electronics! Fuck you Mr. Jobs, and Murdock, and Gates, and Apple Music, and Google Chrome, and Amazon Prime, and YouTube, and you, too, God, for programming in dependence in the damn love program! Is it a feature or bug?

25

PLACE YOUR ORDER

There is far more to astrology than reading a two-sentence horoscope for your birth sign. That's like saying all you need to know in order to write a book is how to hold a pen. I am acquainted with this esoteric science, having participated in a two-year internship program over twenty-five years ago. I'm a big proponent of researching something before dismissing it, especially something that's been around for 5,000 years. As a result, I view the night sky and its language through a lens of opportunity rather than one of prediction. Think of a traffic camera informing the public of current accidents and heavy traffic, or a weather forecast predicting snow tomorrow. If you have somewhere to be, you might want to readjust your travel plans accordingly.

As it happens, there is to be a total lunar eclipse tomorrow night. It would be a grand thing to witness and a perfect time to make a wish or set an intention. In a nutshell, eclipses have to do with endings and beginnings, depending upon whether it occurs during a new or full moon. The one tomorrow will be a full moon lunar eclipse—think super moon—which amplifies feelings and speeds things up towards completion. Setting an intention during that window would be a great opportunity to tie things off, so to speak, like a window of time wherein one could avoid traffic jams and snowstorms when traveling.

Eleven years ago, in 2008, the first time I visited Boca, there was another night sky on resplendent display as well, a once-in-a-decade alignment of planets forming what is called a grand cross. It was a moment during which I put in my order to the Universe, declared my intention, and damn if I didn't get it. In light of Christina's impending death and my own internal unrest regarding my obvious dependence on electronics and the weaning from same, not to mention from Christina, I feel I should make *some* note of the event, set some sort of intention. I should ask for something, anything, and at least pay attention. Because this eclipse is about endings and my friend lies in a room above me, dying. It feels obvious, like an invitation, but for the life of me, I cannot think of a single thing I want beyond Christina not dying, and I know that's not a possibility. She will die. Her body will give out. But her spirit? In my world, that's ensured already, so no need to ask for that.

I sit on my veranda and stare out into the night sky dotted with brilliant sparks of light. There are thousands more stars visible to the human eye up here on the mountain above this tiny seaside village than there are in Toronto. The sounds of life float my way: little-girl giggles, music from someone's window, chickens clucking, dogs barking. There is an overriding sense of community in this town, a blanket of peace tucked under its chin.

Peace! That's what I want! Peace. I want Christina to pass peacefully. I am suddenly alive, plugged in, as though I was digging for treasure and just struck the chest. This *feels* right, it feels real. I want peace for my friend. Done. My order is placed.

And then a moment later, a nagging finger: *And what about you? That's for her. What do you want for you?*

Uh, oh. *You're right.* And so, I continue to sit and stare out into the dark. I sit there for at least an hour. It seems it should be simple, figuring out why you really want, but it's not, not if you take time to determine *why* you want what you think you want.

Before I go to bed, I figure it out.

In the training biz, there's a concept called *la ligne rouge*, the red line, the unifying order to the consistency and flow of a learning environment: *This* idea leads to *this* exercise, which leads to *that* learning, and then I move the group on to the next concept, and on it goes until the learning objectives for the workshop are met. Sitting here in the dark, I suddenly see, in crystal clarity, the red line of my life—the turning points and people who were there and why. It all makes sense to me in this moment, how the pieces of my life fit together. My unique unifying concept, *la ligne rouge*.

Though the full moon eclipse itself is not for twenty-four more hours, I look into the sparkling night sky and declare my desire. I want peace for me, too, inside and out. I want it enough to make future choices *for* it, having made too many against it in the past, like hanging on to hurts, regrets, and resentments. I vow to make active choices *for* it moving forward. I promise to protect myself —my body, mind, and spirit—as rigorously as Christina safeguards her energy. I will seek peace in my life like a thirsty man seeks water. Every cell in my body relaxes in relief, and I realize it's all I've ever wanted.

I make a deal with the energy field I call God or the Universe. My use of those words is not to be confused with a god of religion, or one of vengeance and fear, but rather the One Beyond, that which religions attempt to interpret, reducing their god to the size of their fears. But mine is bigger than that. It is far larger than the four walls of a church. Mine is one of energy, of love, light, and creation from which I believe all things spring, and which is available to me at any time.

So, I agree to be an active participant in the peace process, particularly as it relates to self-protection (I still lean, like any good adult child of an alcoholic, towards being overly-responsibile and caring for others instead of myself) while She handles Christina's end, a peaceful end. There is a sort of silent understanding: *Leave me to do Christina — you do you. Go forth and trust.*

People say they just want to be happy, but I suspect that's a misnomer, and one usually based on external circumstances. I think, perhaps, peace is what people seek. And I think maybe peace is the opposite of pain, the flip side of the acceptance coin, to feel content without complacency, purposeful devoid of pushiness.

I sleep well that night. Really well. Noticeably well. When I wake, something feels . . . different. It is as though someone snuck in and moved my bed during the night. When I open my eyes, my perspective is altered. The power of words — and clarity. In hindsight, it's a good thing I took the time to sit there and stare at all those brilliant stars, pondering my red line. Today, the sky is covered in heavy, dark clouds, obscuring any view of God's roadmap.

It pays to pay attention. It pays to take advantage of opportunities when they're presented, not when they are supposedly scheduled.

26

WHAT'S COOKING, KIDDO?

The kitchen is alive with activity when I arrive to refill my coffee cup the next morning. Christina has awakened with an appetite. Alesia cooks eggs at the stove while Joy helps Christina with her shower. The showers are becoming fewer, and each takes longer from bed to shower and back.

"Hey." I announce my arrival to Alesia's back.

"Hey!" She turns, smiling. She holds a spatula in her right hand. "Good morning." She's wearing yoga pants and a sleeveless cotton top that crisscrosses in the back. There is an apron tied around her waist, which paradoxically covers as well as accentuates the slight belly bulge above and below it. Her long brown hair is piled atop her head and held in place by a large clip from which a few errant strands dangle. She oozes warmth and safety. Nurture is her middle name. She is Mother Earth incarnate.

"What are you doing?" I ask, moving to the pantry where a fresh pot of coffee sits on the shelf.

"Getting breakfast together for Christina. I'm trying to cook eggs." Alesia returns to her frying pan. Over her shoulder she adds, "Will you fry some bacon? Christina wants *bacon* with her eggs this morning." Her emphasis on the word *bacon* indicates her disgust in addition to the inside joke. Neither Alesia nor Joy will touch bacon, it being meat and all. Like Joy, Alesia is a vegetarian. She also shares Joy's germ phobia. She cleans everything as soon as a crumb or smudge is seen.

"Sure thing," I reply. "I'm a champion bacon cooker." But my bacon station is occupied. Alesia has taken over the stove and appropriated Christina's mother's perfect fry pan. *This is why they invented microwaves*, I think, *for quick bacon sizzling*. That, plus warming cups of coffee.

Alesia has put some of her sweet bread on a plate and put the plate on a tray. This is the pretty part of Christina's daily routine. Alesia has added a small vase with flowers to the tray, something neither Joy or I have thought to do.

I grab a stack of thick paper dinner plates—from Costco, of course—and tear off sections of paper towel to cover the bacon and absorb the grease. It is not as authentic a method for cooking bacon as frying it in a pan, but it's quicker and easier and keeps the bacon away from Alesia who most definitely wants it kept far away from her. I take the package of thawed bacon—which needed to be cooked anyway—out of the refrigerator and put it into the sink—no raw bacon on Joy's kitchen counter. I cut the plastic away and remove the slimy pieces from their sheath. Alesia eyes me with distaste. Then I cut the bacon strips in half and begin laying them neatly onto the paper towel-covered plates. That way, they fit better and cook evenly in the microwave. When using a pan, don't *ever* cut the strips in half. It's like a man in cold water; there's a shrivel factor. I told you, I'm the Bacon Master.

"Do these look done to you?" Alesia turns from the stove to reveal her efforts.

Two fried eggs sit crammed in the pan. The yolks are a sunflower yellow and the whites are dangerously opaque. These puppies aren't just done, they're dead. You could use the rubbery result as a frisbee. "I've never fried eggs before," she adds, as if I couldn't tell.

"Um, yeah. They're done," I say, and give her a look. Last week I fried eggs for Christina only to have her inform me of her preference for a runny yolk, which I had not provided. "They might be a bit overdone. Christina likes her yolks a little runny. She likes to break them open and smother the white in yolk." I laugh. "I don't get it. I don't eat fried eggs myself."

"I'll try again." Alesia is earnest in her intent.

"I wouldn't worry about it," I reply. She also leans toward anxiety.

"No," Alesia says firmly. "She's hungry. She's dying. She can have what she wants." And then she adds, as though to herself, "I can do this." She scrapes the overdone eggs from the pan into Maya's dog bowl next to the sink. It's Maya's lucky day.

She retrieves two fresh eggs from the fridge. *Why two?* I think. Christina can only eat one, if that. While Alesia takes her second run at the perfect fried egg, I start lining bacon strips on plates; I've gone into production. Alesia has gotten diverted with something. She wanders to and from spaces putting things away. We chat amiably. I begin popping bacon-covered plates into the microwave, one after the other.

Seeing as how neither Joy nor Alesia will touch leftover raw bacon, I see no point in cooking only a few strips for Christina's breakfast. I decide to cook it all. I'll wrap the leftovers for future mornings; Joy will touch cooked bacon. I begin and quickly determine the best time per plate (with six slices strategically placed just so) is exactly four minutes. Times five plates. The bacon will be cooked in twenty minutes.

"Dammit!" Alesia interrupts my calculations. "I broke the yolk."

"No worries. Christina won't care."

"But *I* do!" she says sternly.

This one goes into Bella's bowl: equal opportunity failures.

She still speaks in a soft tone, but I can tell that Alesia is tighter than when she arrived. It's not solely Christina's illness, nor even Joy's anxiety about it, it is her children; Alesia misses her children. She's been gone from them for almost a week, and part of her, right now, is cooking for her kids. She wants to get it right.

I take a minute to show Alesia how to crack the egg such that the egg yolk doesn't break. She tries again. The yolk breaks.

"Fuck."

This is becoming a fabulous day for the dogs.

Joy strides into the kitchen and announces, "Seven minutes. She'll be ready for breakfast in seven minutes. We're done with the shower. I've got to go put lotion on her. I'm just getting some coffee." Joy is moving at warp speed.

I lean on the wall next to the microwave, my handy-dandy stack of bacon laden plates next to the sink, waiting, hanging out. I suddenly feel extremely calm beside these two ladies. The eggs might be fucked, but my bacon is perfect.

"How's it going?" Joy wants to know if we're on schedule.

My bacon is.

"This is my third attempt." Alesia opens the refrigerator to get another egg.

"Maybe just one," I insert. "She'll only eat one."

"Yeah, one will do it," Joy confirms. She glances at the pan. "Add more oil. Cook it halfway and then flip it over." Joy is all business.

Alesia freezes, egg in hand, then turns to Joy with a look of consternation. "Flip it?"

Even from behind, watching their exchange from the fringe of the kitchen, leaning against the wall, I can see Alesia stiffen. Joy's energy is not helping things. Flipping had not been discussed. Alesia doesn't know *anything* about flipping.

"Here. I'll do it." Joy reaches for the egg.

"No!" Alesia raises the egg above her head out of Joy's reach. She stands a good six inches taller than Joy. "I can do it! Go put lotion on Christina."

I stand there, observing it all. *Yes*, I think, *you go do your job and let us do ours.* But I say nothing.

Joy turns away. She grabs her coffee cup and fills it, relights a half-smoked cigarette that languishes in a shell ashtray on the kitchen counter, sits down, and sips her coffee. She takes three drags of her stubby cigarette and then puts it out again. Two minutes have passed since she barked seven minutes. Alesia has successfully broken one egg into the hot pan without breaking the yolk. I'm on the next-to-last plate of bacon. The egg is almost ready. Alesia and I were doing just fine before the micromanager arrived. We're on schedule. Joy is not.

Ding. I remove the grease-soaked paper plate from the microwave, and with a practiced swivel, replace it with the final plate. I have already stacked the used plates one atop the other, ready to be shoved into the trash can. Several strips—perfectly cooked, I might add —have already been placed on Christina's plate awaiting the arrival of an egg. Alesia has added a small bowl of fruit to one side.

Joy scrolls through her phone. Another minute. Silence, save the sizzling of the eggs and the whirl of the microwave. I glance at the clock. *Four minutes. Damn. Me and the time thing.*

Joy slaps her phone down on the counter and leaps from her chair. She strides around the counter where it curves toward the wall, the wall where I'm leaning. There's maybe three feet between the wall and the counter at this exact spot. Two people have to turn sideways to pass each other through this space. I watch Joy move toward me, her eyes lowered. I'm looking right at her, daring her to lift her eyes. She walks in front of me and has to turn a bit to avoid my lounging form, which I find slightly pleasurable. Not in a mean, vengeful way, but more in a *get over yourself* sort of way. Joy is wound up.

She puts her mug in the sink. She sees the bacon wrapper.

"Jesus Christ. Fucking bacon. What a mess!" She picks the wrapper up between two fingers, at one corner as though holding the tail of a dead mouse, and swivels towards the trash can. I intended to clean everything up after I finished this final plate. I intended to wipe the counter and remove the wrapper from the sink, where it still oozed its poisonous bacon slime. It is still there because the trash can is full.

"Joy, I'm on it," I say. "You don't need to do that. Let me finish with the bacon and I'll clean it all up." Joy is becoming frenetic, brittle.

The trash can, as Alesia has already pointed out to me, is overfull and requires assistance to remove it. It is too full to squeeze even one grease-covered plate into it.

Joy sees the overstuffed, oversized can and swivels back to the sink, disgust written all over her face.

"Crap! This should have been emptied yesterday."

It's time. I confront her firmly. "Joy. Go back downstairs. Go put lotion on Christina. You're wasting time. You're wasting *Christina's* time. We've got this under control." I feel strangely calm. My voice reflects that. "You told us 'seven minutes' six minutes ago. We're ready. But now Christina isn't."

"Fuck it. I'll put the damn lotion on *after* breakfast." Joy replies through clenched teeth.

Alesia turns from the stove, pan in hand, eyes cast downward. Conflict is not really in her wheelhouse. "The egg's done." She slides it onto the pretty plate next to the perfect bacon and beautiful bread. She glances at me. "Does it look okay?"

"It's perfect," I tell her. "Great job."

"I'll take it down," Joy declares.

"No. *I'll* take it down. I cooked it!" Alesia's voice raises in pitch and volume. She picks up the tray. They stop and glare at each other, Joy with frustration, and Alesia with determination. Joy is close to breaking.

And then, she does.

"Fine! *You* take it down then. *Fuck!*"

Joy bends down and retrieves a cleaning cloth from under the sink. She grabs a spray bottle of cleaning solution. A torrent of irritations spill from her lips: the trash, the bacon, the eggs, the mess, whatever. Alesia freezes in place in front of the stove, tray held chest high. She looks like a downstairs maid in *Downton Abbey* minus the cute cap, as though at full attention. I stand guard at the microwave door, a languid, leaning lady, awaiting the *ding* of done—so *up*stairs. Joy strides around the kitchen— which isn't really large enough for anyone to stride, but she takes one long step after another, and well, she has short legs. One step to the trash can, then to the refrigerator, then back to the sink. She has her rag in one hand and the spray bottle in the other. She's armed herself and gone into battle, slashing wildly at her perceived enemies: dirt, clutter, and time. *Fucking time!* Spraying and wiping and striding and venting, she wheezes her resentments like she's playing an accordion with ferocious gusto.

"And I mean, what the fuck is *this*?" She sees dirt and germs everywhere. The kitchen contains an invasion of imaginary infections. She wipes down the door handle and then the front of the refrigerator.

"Her immune system is *compromised*. I *told* you. We need to keep this place *clean*!" Joy's a wee warrior loosed on the battlefield of control. And she's losing, and she knows it, which makes it worse.

Alesia and I catch each other's eye. A raised eyebrow of understanding passes between us. This eruption has been a long time coming. For a full minute it flows. She's angry and tired and wound as tight as an eight-day clock.

And then she's gone. Down the stairs. Suddenly. A scalpel-like exit if ever I saw one.

Ding. The last of the bacon.

I nod at Alesia, still frozen in place holding the breakfast tray. "Take it on down. While it's still warm."

She nods back and gives me a small smile, takes a step, and then stops. "To tell you the truth, I'm not surprised." I remove the last load of bacon from the microwave and snap the door shut.

"Me neither."

"And I'm glad." She turns her head and looks me in the eye. We talked about this a few days ago. We talked about Joy being ready to blow. "She needed that. She needed to release that energy." Mother Earth is also a yoga master.

"Yeah. She did. It's a good thing. I'm glad it was with us." I move to the sink. "You go on down to Christina. I'll clean up." I turn on the faucet and pick up the sponge. "I'll check in with Joy when I'm done here. She needs a few minutes."

A few minutes later, I head down the stairs after Joy, checking the veranda off of her bedroom. She's not there. She's not with Alesia in Christina's bedroom either. I head outside and find her in the garden at the table. She is checking her phone and smoking a cigarette. Her body is bent over at the waist, elbows on her knees. Her head is lowered. She scrolls through the feed on the phone, probably WhatsApp.

"Hey," I say quietly. I sit down across from her and lean my elbows on the table.

She glances at me, briefly, before returning to her phone, and after a beat, says "Sorry."

I wait a beat as well before responding. "Me, too." Soft voices.

Joy takes a drag from her smoke and leans back in her chair. Her eyes are guarded and dart about like one of the homeless dogs she so often rescues from the street. She exhales. It's more a heavy sigh.

"I don't know what happened." She sounds confused.

"Yeah," I say in a measured voice. "Meltdown. I've had a few myself. They're messy, man, just ask my family. A sign of my deep and abiding love." I chuckle. "Listen. You're overwrought, overworked, and over-whelmed." I lean toward her. She returns to her slumped position. "This is a huge task you've undertaken, Joy, a Herculean endeavor, to walk a woman to her death, holding her hand, especially one you love so deeply, so fiercely."

Silence. "And you know how important this is, right? On multiple levels."

"Yeah." Joy nods her head once and then shakes it imperceptibly. "But, man, I thought I was doing so well."

"You are," I assure her. "You are. But you can't control everything, Joy. It's impossible. No one can. And you're the point person, the turnstile. It takes a toll."

I reach out and grab her pack of smokes, lift it with raised eyebrows in the silent universal gesture of request known to smokers worldwide.

"Sure. You deserve it," Joy waves her hand, sits up and gives me a slight smile.

We sink into silence while I light the cigarette.

"Here's the thing, Joy." I say. It's my time to talk now, to guide, to be the big sister. It's in the tone of my voice and I know it and she does, too. She expects it: an extended hand.

"You're not just letting Christina go," I continue. "You're letting your mother go, all over again. I know you know that, at least intellectually. Only this time, you're doing it as an adult, with your eyes wide open. You're doing it consciously, intentionally, emotionally aware. That's *painful*, sweetie. It's fucking painful. That's why people avoid it like the plague."

I take a drag on my cigarette. Joy reaches for a fresh one. "But that pain, that pain of awareness and conscious choice, is the pain of a wound healing. Yours. And this is you, healing, now, from an event that changed the course of your life over thirty years ago. Your mom left without saying goodbye. She took her own life. She denied you the opportunity to say goodbye, to tie off the incredible loss an innocent little girl suffered so many years ago. You've been angry at her, without giving yourself permission to feel it, or express it, and thereby integrate and heal from it. And now, here you are. You've created an opportunity to say goodbye! At last. How incredible is that?"

I lean back in my chair, my body instinctually reflecting the shift from forthrightness to friendship. "Sunshine and butterflies," I continue, "that's you. Your soul—your *essential what-ness* as Aristotle called it—is a vital openness to life, Joy. What did you label it at the program?" I'm referring to the end result of the Joy Class which is to put a name to your soul's mission.

"Gypsy Jewel of Generosity," she replies. Her voice has softened. "I live it every day."

Her words hang there a moment.

"Gypsy Jewel of Generosity," I parrot. My lips curve into an appreciative grin. "And you're living it right now, with Christina." I pause, reflecting on my intermittent but intertwined journey with Joy this lifetime.

"You can't not be who you are, Joy. Everywhere. All the time. And more than anyone I know your essence is love. It just is. I mean, we all are, yes, at our core, but not all of us are so free in our giving of it. In your case it's *all* of you, inside and out. And that's a potentially precarious place to be, so wide open and vulnerable to the vicissitudes of life—to be willing to be tossed around in such a turbulent, uncertain sea. It's one reason—perhaps the main one—why so many people refrain from loving more fully. The pain of potential loss. You? Not so much. You've always been wide open. And that's why I confronted you upstairs. Because that's what I'm seeing dissipate, your vulnerability, your open eagerness."

Joy stares at me. She is listening intently. Her eyes have softened around the edges. The darting has departed.

"I remember the first time I saw you," I continue. "The first time we met for Jenny and Joe's wedding. Remember?"

"Yeah. That was a happy time." Joy smiles. "Bro Joe." She adores her older brother.

My voice softens to the tone of a mother reading her child a bedtime story. "I remember the exact moment I first saw you, standing at my front door with your Dad, your ten-year-old blue eyes looking up at me, all wide-eyed wonder and open eagerness. You were a bright light of unconditional love despite the loss of your mother only a year before."

Joy's eyes well with tears.

"And it pains me to see that light, that openness, diminish through the burden you've chosen to shoulder. Because you don't have to shoulder it *all*, Joy. You don't. Maybe learning how to share the load is part of the point for you, releasing at least some control." Joy is silent, her gaze now averted.

"And where's God in all this, huh? I mean, this comes down to trust, honey. Do you believe you have a partner? That the Universe is in your corner? That this whole thing, this one segment of your life's tapestry, this march toward death holding Christina's hand, is being woven for a purpose? And one that may be beyond your grasp right now? Beyond mine? And to surrender to that, simply trust in that? I mean, why not, Joy? If only to relieve the pressure, whether it's true or not, why not reach out and ask for a little help right now—from the energy you *can* see, like me and Alesia and Isabel, and the energy you *can't* see as well. It's there. You and I both believe that. All you have to do is ask," I finish.

"Yeah. I do believe that." Joy says. Her eyes return to mine. It's time to lighten the mood.

"Because if you don't," I add, "well, that's the beginning of brittleness, baby. And you? Brittle? That's more than I can handle. Because you're *love* and love doesn't break, Joy, it bends."

Tears have spilled their banks in both our eyes. "I love you, Joyous," I finish, using one of her nicknames.

"You're my littlest sister. Please don't let your extraordinary light fade. Christina needs it. And control? It gets in the way, baby. It blocks the beams of love."

I stub out my cigarette and Joy wipes her eyes. "Thanks, sistah," she says and smiles. "Love you, too."

We rise from the chairs and hug. We're complete. "Let's go back inside," I say, shooting her an impish look, "and see if Christina has managed to eat any of that fucking fried egg."

27

LIKE A HOSTAGE

The question has morphed from *when will I see my laptop* to *will I ever see it again*?

I don't want to seem like a pushy white bitch from up north, but I'm close to letting the one I keep on hand out from behind the locked bars in my basement. She can be a very handy ally in a street fight. *In case of fire, break glass.* I have suffered through separation and withdrawal symptoms and (sort of) overcome them. I leave in five days, dammit! I want my laptop returned, dead or alive. I want the body back so I can bury it.

I resist the impulse to tap out a *Hey, where the hell is my laptop?* message to Israel first thing Monday morning, opting instead for a far more politically correct late morning message:

"Hola, Israel. I hope you had a great weekend. Any chance you can tell me when I might see my laptop again? I leave on Thursday and want to plan my final days. Thanks!" There's nothing pushy or bitchy about that. Nope, it's just slightly dishonest. I leave Friday, not Thursday. It's like a margin in gambling—you have to be a little loose with the truth to ensure timely delivery on occasion. Mexican time, *mas tardes*, can mean an hour, a day, or a week.

Later, when I communicate my frustration to Christina, her first response is to ask if I told him I was leaving Friday.

"No, I told him Thursday," I tell her.

"Good." She nods her head once, strong, pauses, and then adds, "I would have told him Wednesday."

She's right, I probably should have told him Wednesday. Honesty has its place, but not when you're negotiating with a stranger holding your baby hostage.

~

Christina asks Joy for a bit more lotion. She looks at me with a wry smile. "More for the massage, the touch, than the dryness," she says. A needless explanation. I don't care what she wants or when she wants it or why. Whatever she wants, she can have.

"How's the pain?" I ask, already knowing the answer.

Her eyes are closed. "Not good."

"Do you want me to get the towel?" Joy has already removed it from under Christina's legs. She is endlessly efficient when replacing things back to *where they belong*.

Christina seems to grimace internally and gives a slight shake of her head. It's the pain. Her voice becomes small. "I don't care." Normally, she would. Normally, she would certainly care about a towel under legs so as not to get lotion on the bedspread. Her head rolls to her left and she looks at me.

"You can tell I'm in pain when I just don't care." She rolls her head back to center. Joy continues to rub lotion onto Christina's calves and feet using long, firm strokes. Christina's eyes close. She is busy trying to enjoy the feel of fingers on her flesh, even as she tries to fight the pain, the relentless pain.

Yes, I can tell she's in pain. I can tell at a glance, in the fraction of an eye movement, a flick of a finger. I can tell that she doesn't care, that she *can't* care any longer. It takes too much energy to care about things that don't matter, energy she mustn't divert from facing the pain, fending it off, talking it down, keeping it below the nose line, when she can't breathe. Like a hungry wolf who's caught her scent, pain is on her trail and she has only enough strength left for combat, not caring. It takes a lot of energy to stay in the ring with severe pain. There's no room to care about protecting some insignificant bedspread from possible creamy stains. There is no room for small decisions any longer. She's done.

The next morning, I knock lightly on Christina's closed door and poke my head around the corner. "Hey! How 'ya doing?"

She shakes her head, answering my question nonverbally.

"Oh, no. What's going on? Did you have a bad night?" I step into her room, close the door behind me, and move to her bedside.

She takes a breath. "Just so you know," she says, right hand over her heart, "I'm having a bad day. There's —" she begins and then closes her eyes tightly. Her face contorts. This happens every day now, and more frequently during each day. She takes a deep breath and focuses. "Okay. There's this pain in my left leg . . . it's becoming normal . . . the pain . . ." She trails off, and then, ". . . it's becoming normal." There is a note of defeat in her voice.

I get her a pain pill. It's an hour early. So what? I can
tell when the pill kicks in; her speech slows, and words
seem just out of reach. Her face relaxes. There are long
pauses as her attention is drawn to some small artifact,
some sidelong movement by gecko or bird or branch of
tree. She is easily distracted from conversation. She
wanders. Apparently, this is common whilst in the
Shadow Valley.

The doctor is coming today. The pain is increasing,
inexorably, toward an end, a numbed, morphine directed
end to her pain, and her life along with it. There will be
no more BLTs, no more good days, only slightly less bad
ones. Her door will stay closed more often.

I am outside reading, sitting at my post in the garden
when the doctor arrives, and I usher him inside.
Christina greets him warmly. The doctor is in his mid-
forties, I estimate, dark-haired, with warm, brown eyes
and a rounded belly pressing against his pale blue,
button-down, short-sleeve shirt. There are perspiration
stains under his arms from the taxing climb up Casa la
Ventana's endless stairs.

I take my place near the doorjamb, with the spiral
notebook in which Joy chronicles Christina's daily functions: food intake, bowel movements, mood, and medications—how often and how much. These are now the
ledger entries of her life. Christina's chronicle. Joy and
Alesia are having dinner down on the beach and I want
to make sure I write down anything of importance, the
doctor's instructions. Joy will want to know.

The doctor examines Christina, takes her blood
pressure and temperature, and then sits in the big
brown recliner. He asks Christina about her newest

symptoms, her pain level, and her regimen of treatments. She asks him about the potential of another nerve block.

"No," the doctor replies. "It can't be done again." One is all she can have, and she had it a month ago. Christina already told me she couldn't have another. I asked her. She's forgotten—or hope has obscured her memory.

The doctor explains that the tumor is growing, that its new tendrils of cancerous growths cannot be deterred in their relentless assault on her insides. That is the pain she feels, he explains, the *new* growth, not the awakening of the largest tumor at the base of her spine, but rather its extensions.

It has not been a good day and she has hung on in the hope that he would carry with him in his bag some sort of catharsis, some pain reduction concoction. Christina is calm and collected during the entire visit. If Joy oozes love and enthusiasm, Christina oozes calm and collected. She is dignified, regal, yet real. She gazes out the veranda doors while the doctor talks. I can see her sorting his information in her head, methodically examining the data, determining where to file it, where it fits in the time that remains.

The time that remains.

My throat tightens. I have only a few precious days remaining with my special sistah. *Fuck time!* And she may only have a few days left herself. When she asks, obliquely, about how long she might have, the doctor answers obliquely, too, with a standard "It's hard to say." Christina turns her eyes back to the veranda doors. Her right hand moves to her head.

"I've noticed some new bumps on my head," she tells him.

The doctor pushes himself up from the chair, extends

his right hand, and feels her scalp. Christina's hand guides his.

"Si. Estos son nuevos." He shrugs and tilts his head. He knows. It can't be stopped. Cancer's army is well trained. He reaches for his bag and reverts to English.

"When it gets to that point, we can look to a morphine drip." He doesn't define what *that* point is, or when it will become evident, but I suspect it's a few days from death, when cancer storms the castle and the gates fall, when pain plants a victory flag and the flesh surrenders.

The doctor writes her a new prescription and hands it to her. She hands it to me. I put it inside the notebook where I've jotted down his new instructions. He rises to leave, slings his bag over his shoulder, then moves back to her bedside. He takes her left hand in his right, covers it with his left, and smiles down at her gently.

"It will be alright. We will take care of your physical needs. You focus your energy on only what you enjoy. I know the pain is hard. We will do our best to manage it." He releases her hand. She gives him a small smile.

"Thank you, doctor. I appreciate you making the trip." Christina is tired.

I show him out and, despite knowing better, ask him a stupid question. I know it's stupid, I know it's unanswerable, and I don't even know why I'm asking, but I ask anyway. It makes me feel proactive somehow, in the face of cancer that's not even mine. As I said, stupid.

"Have you any idea how long she has? A best guess?"

He stops and gives me a kind smile. "There's no way of knowing, really. But I would say weeks, not many, not months. It won't be long."

My head nods once, then twice. "Okay. Thanks." My jaw tightens.

As if sensing my feelings of impotence, he reaches out and touches my forearm. "We will make sure her pain is made manageable." It is a small comfort, knowing someone with a medical bag will tend to her end, but hardly enough warmth to ward off the chill of death's approach that I can feel in my bones.

When I return to her bedroom, Christina's eyes are closed. She seems to have already fallen asleep, exhausted by the doctor's visit. I stand there, holding the doorknob a moment before closing the door, quietly, and tiptoeing down the stairs to my room.

Pain is exhausting. It is exhausting for the injured, but also for those who care for them. Christina is held hostage by her pain. It sends ransom notes every day. She holds her breath and hopes for some relief, some release, and the prospect of another day. She hopes for one more day—a pain-free day.

But those days are behind her now.

The carefree days of youth and invincibility were only an illusion.

28

A MERRY MERYL LIFE REVIEW

L ong ago, and far away, in what feels like another lifetime—before DVDs and downloads—Christina and I went to the movies in Lutherville, Maryland, the suburb where we both lived at the time. This was in 1991, before I had been introduced to Dr. Weiss's book, *Many Lives, Many Masters*. We saw *Defending Your Life* starring a much younger Meryl Streep and Albert Brooks. It was a marvelous romp through an imaginary afterlife experience wherein the two main characters review their respective lives and what lessons they learned while they lived. Meryl had all these heroic, happy life scenes that the review committee—called Big Brains—chose for her to see from their perspective, which revealed her generous, trusting heart. Meanwhile, poor, anxious Albert had to punch rewind on times when he was bullied and didn't stand up for himself.

We found it hysterical, and it *was* a comedy, but I suspect the acid we dropped right before we entered the theatre might have had something to do with it. It wasn't a powerful dose, but it was enough. It might have been a much less amusing film than we gave it credit for, but for

years, up until the very end of her life, Christina and I
hoped to get the Meryl version of a life review.

That was the only time we did LSD together, and
boy, what a time it proved to be. It was a summer Saturday. My marriage was crumbling, my sense of self with
it, and I felt lost and out of control. Christina swooped
in. "Get a babysitter," she told me. "I'm coming to get
you. We're taking the day off." She was used to being in
charge of projects, and she took charge of me, too. I
needed it.

I don't remember who chose the movie, it was probably a function of what was showing, and where, and at
what time, more than it was a desire to see that particular
movie. But it was a perfect choice for us at the time and
we referred to it often throughout the years, like opening
a memory box and gently stroking an ancient memento.

Being that I was an extremely inexperienced acid
dropper, the effects of whatever she handed me prior to
the movie, saying *take this*, lasted until after the movie
ended. I sat there and stared at the rolling credits,
mesmerized, until Christina grabbed my arm and made
me move; she was hungry. We exited the theatre to find
the sky an odd, ugly color, a puce-greenish-grey I had
never seen before. But Christina had. She had lived in
Texas. She knew the look of a dangerous sky, the kind
that spawns tornadoes. But we were on the northern
fringes of Baltimore, Maryland, for heaven's sake, a
place where tornadoes *never* happen.

Until they do.

Coming after the mind-altering substance, coupled
with an emotion-altering movie, this potentially body-
altering weather event almost put me over a very fragile
edge of reality. Did I mention my marriage was
imploding and I was a mess? The conditions were ripe
for a major meltdown. I remember starting to freak while

watching other people walk in a normal fashion, unrushed, to and from the shops in the outdoor strip mall. Could they not see the sky? Did they not know that something big and very bad was about to happen? Was it only me? Was I *that* high?

Thankfully, it wasn't just me. Christina took charge. Again. She looked skyward and confirmed that, yes, something was up. I was in no condition to argue, grateful that my version of reality and hers seemed to match. Taking me by the shoulders, she steered me across a small, grassy hill and toward the two-story parking garage which offered, according to her, the best protection in case of a tornado. We hovered in a corner as people wandered by, oblivious to the warnings screaming down from above. *Silly people.* Which is, in hindsight, probably what they thought about *us* at the time, two *loco* ladies crouching under the edge of a parking garage. Later, we found out a tornado had indeed touched down only five miles from us, a beyond rare occurrence. The sky hadn't lied. It enabled us to feel smugly self-righteous about our precautions and body positions. It is always reassuring to realize in hindsight that foolish behavior was not wasted effort.

The sky cleared within the hour, as did the effects of the drug, and Christina drove me home. But after all these years, and the many memories we made along the way, we both still cling to the distant desire instilled that day: that we be blessed with a merry Meryl life review.

I suspect that Christina, like the character from the movie Miss Meryl played, will enjoy her review very much. It should be a great show. I'm grateful to have had a supporting role.

29

SO MUCH FOR BOUNDARIES

Joy has gone to the airport with Alesia, who is flying home to her children today. Christina is napping and the front door is locked. I've taken a short break from my guard duties and strayed from my post to my room. It is directly below Christina's; I can hear her if she calls. I am beginning to gather my things together in preparation for my imminent departure. The house is quiet. I sit on the sling-back chair on the veranda off my bedroom. A moment of stillness.

Suddenly, I hear a voice from behind me. Don has entered my room. He has walked right into my room without knocking. That'll teach me to leave my door unlocked.

"Hey," he says and raises a hand in welcome.

I get up and scurry toward him. We converge in front of my bed and I give him an awkward hug of greeting. "Hey, Don. What's happening?"

My phone dings. It's a text from Christina. "Don is banging on the front door. Will you please tell him to go away?" That's not a request, it's an order. How on earth did I not hear him?

"I'm on it," I text her back. "He's in my room now."

"You want some water?" I ask Don, ever the hostess. "I'm afraid that's all I've got."

"Oh, yeah, sure. That's fine."

I retrieve two glasses of water and offer Don a seat on my balcony. A simple question kicks off what turns into a forty-five-minute conversation.

"So, how you been, Don? What brings you by?"

"I'm okay, I guess. I just wanted to see her. That's all. I had a rough day and I just wanted to see my best friend."

"Yeah. I get it. I know this is hard, Don. You love her, and you love this place." I'm being sympathetic and kind in an attempt to validate his feelings, but apparently I might have been better served not to have done so because out it pours, all the hurt and pain and confusion. All the anger and fear and frustration. How he's been slighted. How life's done him wrong. How Christina owes him access. How he's lonely. How the world is out to get him. I offer input, here and there, every suggestion batted away with why it wouldn't work, or how he's already tried that, or why it's a dumb idea. Linear thought is outside his grasp; circular is all he knows now.

Finally, I feel full. I've grown weary of his conversational wandering.

"Well, listen, Don, I really do need to finish this up, and think about something for dinner." Subtlety is not one of my strengths. I may as well have said, "Time to go."

"Give her a hug and kiss for me." He may have understood my message, but he makes no move to leave.

"Yes, I will give her a hug and kiss for you." Maintaining eye contact, I will him to rise from his chair and move toward the door.

"And ask her when a good time would be to come by and tell her to email me." He stays glued to his chair.

My response is automatic. I don't even pause. "No." Swift and firm, as though a dog is sniffing meat on the counter. "No, Don, you don't get to put it onto *her*. It's up to *you* to reach out, not her." I am suddenly focused.

"Well, *you* do it then." He sounds like a stubborn little boy.

"No, no, no—"

"*You* do it. I don't—"

"No, Don. That's not my responsibility, it's yours."

"I don't see why. I've tried—"

"No, Don. Stop." I raise my right hand like a traffic cop. "Do you see how you're shirking responsibility? She was clear. No response to an email means 'No, don't stop by.' You're supposed to call, anyway. That's what we agreed to last time you stopped by."

"I've tried. And I *am* taking responsibility. I *do* email. Nothing comes back. The internet here—it's so bad—and nothing comes back! So, I stop by. Big deal. What would *you* do?"

He's becoming frantic so I try to calm my voice. "You have a phone, Don. *Call* if the internet's out. We talked about this last week."

His tone changes immediately. His eyes become hooded. "I'll just fucking show up then," he hisses at me. Animals of all kinds lash out when cornered or caught. Limping has become his norm. It has crippled his capacity for joy.

I lean forward, toward him, my elbows sinking to my thighs, and clasp my hands together in front of my knees.

"No, Don," I reply gently. "You *won't*. Because you will find the front door locked." I look into his eyes and summon all the scalpel-like compassion I can find. *Measure twice, cut once.*

"I know this is painful, Don. I do. It's painful for all of us. But it's no longer about you, or me, or Joy, or anyone else. It's about Christina. She gets to make the rules now. She gets to determine who she'll spend her remaining time with."

"But I want to see her." Like a child denied dessert, Don is fuming, his face pinched, his eyes narrowed. If he were a cartoon character, steam would shoot from his ears. He is not sad, he is self-righteous and angry, angry with Christina, with me, and with the circumstances. He is angry with life.

"A lot of people want to see her, Don, but if you or I or anyone else deplete her energy, then she has a right to say, 'I don't choose to spend what time I have left with you.' At the beginning of this conversation what you said was, 'I wanted to see her. I had a rough day and I just wanted to see my friend.' What I'm saying is, if that is your true desire, then just showing up here is not the way to get what you want. The way to get what you want—which *you* say is five minutes of her time—is to *call*. Not to email, not text. Call. Earlier, you said your phone was working and then later you said it wasn't, that the battery had died, and you needed to charge it." I'm talking to a ten-year-old.

"I was trying. First it stopped, then it went dead."

"Right. So, there's your lesson. The lesson is to keep your phone charged. Now, if what you're saying to me is that unless *she* emails *you* and tells you it's a good time to visit, then you're going to show up, that's not okay. That's not what we agreed to, Don. What we agreed to was that you would *call*, and your phone *does* work when it's charged, as does Christina's."

"I was forced to agree to this," Don snaps at me. "When you're forced to agree to something, you're not really agreeing to it."

"No, Don, you agreed," I reply. My calm demeanor surprises even me. "Nobody put a gun to your head. That's a convenient argument, a neat way out, but it's not the truth."

"You want truth?" His voice becomes small and whiny; he's reverting to self-pity. "I'll tell you my truth, but nobody wants *my* truth."

"Don, here's the truth as it stands pertaining to the reason you're even sitting here with me right now. You've arrived unannounced and been denied entry. That's the truth. All the rest is extraneous. Christina has laid a boundary and you're saying, 'I understand the boundary, but I'm going to disregard it because I don't like it, don't agree with it, and don't think it's fair.' That's what I'm hearing, Don, and I'm saying, yeah, maybe it's not fair. And who the fuck cares? Lots of things aren't fair, Don, life's not fair. That's not important anymore. If you want to see her you must *call* before you come. You must ask her permission. It's that simple."

Don doesn't respond. He seems to be listening. Perhaps I'm getting through to him. I take a breath and continue.

"It's a simple equation, Don. If you do A you will get B. You want B—five minutes with your friend. To get that you must *call*. That's A. It's pretty simple. But, if you continue to stop by unannounced, you will continue to find the door locked to you. Okay? She keeps the door locked now, for this very reason. I lock it behind me every time I leave the house to avoid unwanted visitors. We lock the door for this exact reason. Showing up out of the blue and banging on the door is not okay, not anymore. It's not okay for anyone. It isn't about you, Don. There need to be clear delineations and boundaries, and I'm sorry that you feel wronged, and I'm sorry you don't get to be here like you want to be, but that's no longer the issue. You have either got to let *that* go, or let *her* go, and not see her anymore, because you don't get to be angry while you're here. You don't get be pissed off at her while in her presence. That's not what this is about anymore, Don. Okay? Not anymore."

I lean back in my chair and let out a deep sigh. I am done with circles and repetition. "Okay, I'm done." The professional switch flicks off. Back to personal mode. "You okay?" I reach out and pat his left thigh.

"Yeah. I'm okay. Thank you." His tone is even. Seems the fight has gone out of him. Maybe my words have reached him.

"Do you get it?" I require confirmation.

He pauses, his eyes on mine. He doesn't blink. "No." It is a small, quiet *no*, empty of anger, full of confusion.

But I'm done. In personal mode I have no more room for anything Don-related. There aren't enough words to help him. "Okay. Well, so here's the deal. I recorded all of that. Just so you can listen to it later."

Don laughs, relieved. "I'll probably need it!" It's the laugh of a scarecrow, hollow and temporary. I walk him to the door and then to the steps leading down to the pool.

"Take care of yourself, Don."

"Oh, I will," he trills over his shoulder. "You do the same."

I stand for a short moment and watch him make his way down the stairs. He has probably forgotten the conversation already, and I realize that boundaries are utterly ineffective when invisible to the person for whom they were created.

30

LEO KNOWS

It's Wednesday morning. I leave in two days. Israel has yet to reply to my text. I no longer care. Let my laptop return whenever it does. Or not. Let it rot away. I'm prepared to buy a new one back in Toronto if I don't get this one returned before my flight in forty-eight hours. My withdrawal has ended. Anxiety has packed her bags and taken with her any concern that something important might be happening outside my awareness, or even that it's important to chronicle what is. The only thing that matters is happening right here, right now, whatever that may be. Whether it's making Christina's lunch right here in Boca, or listening to a client in crisis back in Toronto, or playing with Peyton at the family cottage, it's all the same. It's as though some gear has slipped into place, some cog unstuck, and my insides have settled into a quieter rhythm.

Is this called peace?

I'm reading my fourth book, having overcome my resistance to electronic reading material by being gifted with a Kindle on my last birthday. I'm a fan now; reading outside is no longer a challenge and it saves precious space in my handbag. *All hail Emperor Amazon and his able servant, King Kindle.* Would I have read *any* books had I had my laptop? Doubt it. Would I have paid as close attention to each moment? No, I would have tried to capture them in print and probably would have missed the ones that mattered. Would my internal clock have slowed enough to notice not only the passage of time, but also its irrelevance? Certainly not.

This separation from my laptop has heightened my powers of observation, fueled my ability to be more fully present each day, more aware. I notice subtle details observing the activity of those around me: microfacial expressions, the shift of a shoulder or shake of a head, the glance of an eye or tightening of a jaw. Repetitive movements and telling ticks, like the way Toto stands still and considers his next move when repairing a closet door; the pride in his voice when he calls out to Christina to declare the job complete; the way Isabel listens, her eyes alert and engaged, waiting for the sound of Christina's voice, in case she might need something; the way Joy ticks off tasks in a tidy, efficient fashion, moving like some diminutive Christmas elf, a logistics manager keeping the huge operation in motion, making sure the pain train stays on schedule.

Traits that I might otherwise find annoying under certain circumstances now appear benign, almost endearing. Underneath it all, everyone's just doing the best they know how, every day, just to get through that day. And the fact that some people's behavior on some occasions may not rise to my standards is completely beside the point; that has nothing to do with anything. The only thing that matters is seeing the good. Christina's teaching me that, to look harder for the good, especially in people. And in myself, too, to be kinder to me, something I have not done easily or well for too long. But I'm beginning to allow myself to feel content with who I've become, to allow the small pleasures, to not wait for special occasions to use the good china, to not need a reason to buy a friend a gift, or write a note, or eat the chocolate. It's best to do those things now; waiting for later is a lousy way to get there faster.

After coaching and conducting so many workshops, after all the study and speeches, I am well trained in the art of subtle data gathering and dissemination. I'd say I'm a fairly observant person, at least most of the time. But this level of awareness is new; it's deeper than the body movements and words of the person in front of me. This heightened awareness seems to include plants and animals and energy and intentions in a way more easily felt than seen or heard. The more I notice where I am and what's around me, the less I notice the passage of time. Worry has withered away. I feel like I'm watching the world unfold before me, each day, in slow motion, and sharp focus.

It's like HDL, high definition living.

I mean, who needs a fucking laptop? *Seriously.*

I'm outside, reading at the garden table, guarding the front door again. It's what I do now. No more hovering. Suddenly, the door whips open and Leo's head emerges. He's been visiting with Christina for the past hour and a half. It's been a long stay behind her closed door. I suspect they both know there won't be many more.

"Oh! There you are." He twists his body around and shouts over his shoulder, back to Christina. "She's out here," he shouts. "Guarding the door."

I never told him I'd adopted that role. Leo knows it, though, because he lives it, too, guarding.

"See you later," he calls out to Christina as he closes the door. He turns and grins at me, but there is tightness at the edges of his eyes, and in his smile, a sadness. He knows. He's been here before. He's seen the lengthening shadow cast by a dying sun several times. He knows the look of life's lingering last glance.

I bounce from my seat. "Yep! I be the guard!" We meet in front of the portico. "How was your visit?"

"Great. Always is." Leo is a man of few words. "I heard Don dropped by. *Unannounced.*" Leo has a way of enunciating certain words so that his judgements are made known without needing to actually voice those judgements. If you didn't know Don, you would deduce from Leo's tone alone—and accurately so—that he considers Don an idiot. Leo long ago dismissed him. Don fell into the fool category before dementia danced to the fore. "I heard you gave him a *talking* to." I really had recorded the last seven minutes of the conversation and played it back for Christina, who played it for Joy and Leo. I know she was pleased by it, but I think she might also have been a bit proud of me, too.

"Yeah. He walked right into my room. I couldn't believe it. I could've been naked, man!"

"Well, that would've been a real treat."

We both laugh, once, a way to lighten the sadness of Don's demise and Christina's departure. We both remember when they were a *we* and we all would go for boat rides or stop by Leo's place for a drink. Back when his girlfriend, Brenda, was still alive, and he was happy, and his hip didn't hurt.

"What's this, Leo, your third time?" I didn't need to say, *losing a woman you love.*

Leo holds my gaze. His face reflects a fierce firmness. He lifts his left hand, dramatically, curls his thumb into his palm, and raises the remaining four fingers.

"Four? Jesus, Leo." I look down at my feet and shake my head. "I'm so sorry." Looking back to his face I say, "This must be so hard for you, to lose another to cancer." Leo has lost three women he's loved to this insidious disease, been there all the way with them, or the portions they would allow. His most recent relationship, Brenda, who did love him, but loved her looks more, chose to die back in Canada, and wouldn't allow him to visit. She was a beautiful woman and didn't want his memories of her to hold her wasted frame front and center. Christina told me it broke his heart. Christina will be the fourth person he's loved and lost to cancer. By those standards, I suddenly feel lucky; she's only my second.

"Fucking cancer." I shake my head again. Impotence and head shaking seem to go together like peas and carrots, as Forrest Gump might say. "The pain's getting worse. She says she wants to make it until her birthday, but I don't think it'll happen." My voice trails off. That's two months away, on St. Patrick's Day, March 17th. Leo is silent. We both know it won't happen. Christina knows it, too, but won't say it out loud for fear of making it more real than any of us can stand.

Leo starts towards the stairs. It's time to leave. Just like that, when Leo's ready to go, he goes. When the conversation gets too close, he'll seek distance. These are his default settings.

But he stops after one step, his right hand gripping the handrail. He looks up to the sky and takes a deep breath. I see his chest expand. His eyes close for an instant. He turns his head over his right shoulder and looks back toward me, one leg down, one still on the step above. He exhales. "It won't be long now," he says knowingly.

"May it be a peaceful passing," I say quietly, mostly to myself.

Leo's head snaps front. He nods, once, quickly. "May it be peaceful." And then he starts walking down the stairs again.

"Leo, hang on," I call. "Come back. Give me a hug. I probably won't see you again before I leave." I skitter the few feet from where I stand, to the top of the stairs.

"Leave?" Leo halts his downward trajectory on the third step and turns around at the waist.

"Yeah, unfortunately. I've got stuff back home to attend to. I considered staying. I've been mulling it over for several days. But it's time. We had the May visit. Staying won't make leaving any easier at any time."

His eyebrows shoot straight up. "But you just got here!"

"Actually, Leo, I got here almost three weeks ago. I leave on Friday." I raise four fingers on my right hand. "Four Fridays, Leo. That's all I have." I've told him this before, but it wasn't on a list, so he can't be expected to remember.

"Oh. Well. Okay." He takes a step back up and we hug goodbye. He pats me on the back as he releases me, the thing big men do sometimes when things get real, as though they're patting a child's head reassuringly, or brushing away a fly.

"I'll be back, Leo. Don't worry." I look around Christina's abundant garden, then up to the sky, and finally back to his face. "Being here again has awakened something in me." I smile at him. "I'll see you next winter, if not before."

He turns and continues down the stairs. He's done.

"I'll be here," he says in closing. "You know where to find me."

"Take care of our girl for me," I say to his back. He

raises his left hand and waves his commitment, a verbal confirmation unnecessary. I know him to be a man of his word—whether it be a wave or the middle finger.

I watch from the top of the brick stairway as Leo makes his way down. He grips the heavy iron handrail with his right hand, lurching side to side with each step. I can hear his bad hip screaming at him as he grits his way to the bottom. Bone on bone.

The pain we endure for those we love.

But it's pain with a purpose.

Israel finally responds to my texts. Two days before I leave, on Wednesday evening at 8:05 p.m., he puffs his way up the stairs to Casa la Ventana and hands over the hostage, a hunk of grey metal I no longer consider my baby. I am surprised by how little I care once I hold it. It's not that I've lost my affection for it so much, but I feel detached from it.

Note to self: remember the agony of withdrawal. Don't *ever* become dependent on damn electronics again. They are too fucking transient and irrelevant in the grand scheme of things, when you turn your attention to more meaningful matters.

31

THE DAM BURSTS

The sun has set. The house is quiet. It has not been a good day.

I sit in Christina's leather recliner just watching her, again, just rocking, again. Her eyes were closed when I tiptoed into her room and she didn't stir, so I assumed she was sleeping. As I gaze upon the withered body of my once physically firm friend, I am unable, finally, to stave off the reality of our imminent goodbye. Tomorrow will be our final physical parting. This is our last night, and I know that it is also most likely my last chance to say whatever I need to say to her in order to feel complete when I get on a plane tomorrow, which feels utterly impossible at this moment.

The theme song from the movie *To Sir With Love* leaps into my brain. *Those schoolgirl days* . . . that song always chokes me up and makes me nostalgic for innocence and youth. I don't need any assistance in that direction at the moment, thank you. . . . *but how do you thank someone* . . . I must turn off this song in my head or else I will melt into a puddle right here on the chair. Oscar Wilde said,

"Music is the can opener of the soul." He was a smart guy and good with words, a real wordsmith.

Words.

I cannot seem to summon them, not enough of them, anyway. And not the right ones. What *are* the right words, the ones that could communicate my love for Christina? How *do* I say goodbye? My throat clenches at each new thought of how to begin. Language is so rich and varied and yet we rely on routine and repetition during stressful times. In moments that might matter most, words will often fail us. They are too small for the feelings they try to describe. Even *I love you* seems inadequate, a constricting container for the extent of feelings the phrase represents, the ones flooding me now.

Her left arm, the one closest to me, lays straight and flat on the bed beside her shrinking body. She clutches her phone in her left hand. Every so often, her eyes flutter open and she looks at the screen, but she has yet to acknowledge my presence.

"Waiting for a text?" I finally ask. She doesn't open her eyes but instead flips the phone toward me revealing a stopwatch.

"I'm waiting to poop," she says, her voice a deadened monotone. "Twenty-four more minutes."

This doesn't make sense to me. "Why twenty-four?" I ask.

"Suppository. Takes an hour." She's on the verge of three full days without a bowel movement, and she ate enough yesterday to warrant a decent poop today, but so far, no luck. It's an ongoing issue as the tumor continues its relentless invasion of her private inside space, winding its tentacles around her internal organs, choking the natural excretory processes into submission, and ultimately, defeat. She's down to clipped sentences, evidence of her pain.

My throat keeps clenching. I know if I speak, the logjam will burst, and the volume of feelings released will be loud and crashing. It will be messy, fast, and furious, like a river bursting its banks, flooding the fields. It will be more than she can handle. So, I wait. I will wait until there is a place in between, a place where I can say what I must and not drown its personal significance in a sloppy cathartic mudslide.

Christina glances at her phone. "Seventeen," she says.

I continue to rock, watching her. Why is telling her how I feel so fucking important, anyway? Is it even important? And to whom? And why? What's best for *her*? To data dump my file of meaningful memories at the altar of our past in the midst of her pain? Do I even have the right? Of course I do, I know that, at least intellectually. I can say what I need to, but is it *necessary*? What's my intention? Who's it *for*?

"Twelve minutes."

Each time she opens her eyes, looks at her phone, and announces the time, she closes her eyes again immediately. She obviously isn't interested in interacting. I say nothing, my knees tucked up to my chest with my arms wrapped around them, rocking myself in her lounger. Like lulling a babe to sleep, I am trying to soothe myself into summation mode.

The minutes pass. I keep watching and rocking. I will rock and stay quiet until I can answer my own questions. *So many questions.* I am trying to formulate a clear beginning, middle, and end. If I'm going to try, I'm going to give it my best speaker's effort.

"Seven."

I'm running out of time, or it feels that way. It feels as though now, right now, these few minutes while the house is quiet and Joy is upstairs in the kitchen cooking, is the *only* time I have left with Christina. The fingers of panic start to tickle my gut. *Goddammit! Fucking time!* Christina's impending exit to the bathroom suddenly seems like my last chance for her attention—and my own completion. Just like her physical constipation, if I don't clear my emotional logjam, it'll back up on me. I must squeeze some sensitive, spiritual shit into seven minutes, before she attempts to squeeze out her backed-up physical equivalent.

And then, just like that, my mouth starts moving, and sounds come out. I have no conscious plan for what to say or how. It's been wiped out in the feeling flood. It just happens.

"I have something to say," I begin. "And I've been sitting here wondering if I should say it. And I've decided, yes, I'm going to say it, because I have some things I *need* to say." I take a breath and try to gather my thoughts before continuing. "And because this is our last night and I don't want to try and squeeze it in tomorrow morning. And I want you to listen, even if you don't want to listen, even if you don't need to hear it, because I need to say it."

I get up from the lounger and stand. Like standing when Atticus left the courtroom, or Sir walked into the classroom, you stand for moments like that, for people like that.

Christina opens her eyes and looks at me.

"Hang on. I'll need Kleenex." I skitter to the bathroom, grab a wad of toilet paper, and scurry back to the foot of the bed. I look directly at her. *Okay. I can do this.*

And, the words are there. Suddenly. It's as though my soul steps forward, shoves my poor, sad little self aside, and a lifetime of love begins to pour forth.

"You are the reason I am what I am today," I begin. My throat has relaxed enough to allow words to escape.

"Not the *only* one, but a big one, anyway, not to get all melodramatic about it. You have been there, or available, during many of the most significant moments of my life. So many of them! Had I not met you, had we not become friends, I would not have attended the Pursuit of Excellence. *You* are the reason I attended, not Rob, not my husband's recommendation, but *yours*. I still remember the moment at the introductory session — how you looked, what you were wearing, where you were standing — when I asked you, 'Is it worth it? To sign up?' And you said, 'Best investment I ever made.' And I remember that moment, distinctly, how it felt, and how I didn't even respond to you, I just turned on my heel and marched to the sign-up table, whipped out a credit card and filled out the registration form."

I have traveled thirty years into the past, a sharply defined, bright crystal of a memory as real now as it was then. My throat begins to tighten. I know I will lose this battle soon and be unable to speak at all if I don't get the words out, and quickly.

"If I hadn't taken the Pursuit, I wouldn't have become a facilitator. And I would never have led the Wall. When you flew out to be on my first team . . . that meant so much to me!" I lose the battle. Tears fall from my eyes and I dab at them ineffectually.

"Remember the drive back to the airport afterwards?" I ask her.

"I remember smoking a joint and getting wasted." A full sentence. She's with me.

"And I kept missing the exit for whatever terminal it was. Remember that? There was so much construction. We kept driving around." We both chuckle at the memory. I blow my nose while shuffling to her bathroom to grab more toilet paper.

"Yeah," she says, "and then I get inside the airport

and bump into someone I know." She's got her own version of my memory. "That was weird."

I'm back at the foot of her bed, a fresh supply of tissue in hand and ready for the home stretch.

"What I remember is what you said to me as I drove, before we got to the airport. You said I managed energy in a room better than anyone you'd ever seen. I didn't even know what that meant back then. But I do now, and you were right; I'm an excellent energy manager. But it took years to master. And resting on my faith in *your* opinion, I kept at it. I became the top Wall leader that year. Without *that* I never would have had the confidence to design my own program, to break away and launch my own company. And if I *hadn't*, there would be no Trust Program. And Joy wouldn't have attended. And without The Trust Program, she wouldn't have come to the Joy Class here in *Boca* in 2009. And she and you would never have *met!*" My pitch has raised an octave. *La ligne rouge.* The words are a torrent. I'm a blubbering mess.

"The threads . . ." Christina replies. "We did much of our work together." She returns my gaze. Her eyes are dry. I suspect she's thought all these things already and is allowing me the opportunity to say them to her, not because she needs or even wants to hear them, but because she knows I need and want them to be heard, and loves me enough to summon the energy to listen.

These words suddenly seem to be the most important I've ever uttered. Like standing for an oral exam, the Universe wants to know what I've learned.

"And Joy wouldn't be here now, holding your hand. And just as important, you're holding hers. Letting her have closure and a loving letting go of her own mother, at some level."

Christina nods once, slowly. She's looking at me

hard, completely. "This is important for her as well. For both of us."

"You've been important to a lot of people, sweetie. *Mi tambien*. You are the reason—a key part of it, perhaps the most important part of it—for where I am today, Christina. After the carbon monoxide accident, you showed me a simpler way to live, and what peace and power really mean, and how grace can still be firm, and strength can still be kind . . . and . . . and . . . I just had to tell you. Because I am so utterly and completely grateful. So grateful. You've been a wonderful friend to me, and my only big sister." My face is covered with tears and the tissue in my hands is now a moist mess.

I take a breath and wipe my nose again. Christina glances at her phone.

"Two minutes." She almost sighs as she says it. There's a tone of accomplishment and relief. Here I am, pouring out my heart—it's right *there*, inside out, bleeding all over her bed—and she's announcing T-minus two minutes until poop blastoff! It's too much for me, the disparity on the spectrum of human experience, from the sublime to the ridiculous in a split-second. My knees buckle and I collapse in laughter at the foot of her bed, my upper body flopping face forward onto her bedspread.

"What?" Christina is puzzled.

"I'm baring my soul and you're counting down to poop time!" *It's perfect.*

"I want to poop." *Her priorities.*

"I know! But I'm sorry, the juxtaposition of my heart-based words next to your body-based wants is hysterical."

Laughing as hard and deeply as I think I've ever laughed in my whole life, I head back to the bathroom to toss my soggy wad of tissue into the trashcan and retrieve more toilet paper. I'm not sure I'm done yet, but the spontaneous laughter has sort of seared the incision after my clumsy open-heart surgery. My guffaws have lured Joy downstairs from the kitchen where she is cooking marinara sauce, or trying to. She has never made it before, something Christina and I find unbelievable for a twenty-year vegetarian. She stands in Christina's doorway holding a wooden spoon covered in runny red sauce.

"What's going on, ladies?"

"Nothing much," I say as I finish blowing my nose. "I'm baring my soul and crying and she's waiting to poop."

Joy laughs, too. "How long?"

Christina answers. "One more minute."

"Good. Okay." Joy thrusts the sauce-covered spoon at me. "Here, taste this. How is it?"

I take a lick off the front. "Pretty good. Needs salt. Is there garlic in there?" It needs something, but it is, after all, her first attempt.

"Yeah." Joy turns to Christina. "Want a taste? You're the expert." I hand over the spoon.

Christina takes a taste and hands the spoon back to Joy. "More garlic," she commands. She's right.

Her phone *dings*. She sits, slowly, and lifts the light cover off her legs to make a measured move to leave the bed. Joy and I part like the Red Sea, creating an unencumbered path to the bathroom ten feet away, and she shuffles her way off to a good poop, or so she hopes. Joy begins the nighttime routine, fluffing the pillows and straightening the covers.

"Any luck?" Joy calls. She needs to know poop times.

"I just sat down!" Christina's irritation is evident.

Joy finishes the bed and gets the medication box out

while I blow my nose a final time. She takes off the top and removes the nighttime medication.

"You okay?" She calls over her shoulder to Christina. It's been thirty seconds.

From around the corner Christina says, "I'm *fine*," but the emphasis on the word 'fine' belies its accuracy. "Just let me *poop*."

"Okay."

Joy turns to me and we begin to giggle. It's not funny, but it is. At that moment, Christina's laser focus on moving her bowels, intertwined with my parting words, my elegant summation, my lifetime of love, seem akin to the tumor choking her intestines.

"Maybe we should help her with a cheer, like we used to do at the cottage," I say.

"What cheer?"

"'Push it out, shove it out, *w-a-a-a-y* out.'" I mime along as though I'm a cheerleader holding imaginary pom-poms. Joy joins in. We think this is very funny and add foot movements to our hand choreography. Something has gone askew and we can't stop laughing. We try, but to no avail.

Christina yells at us. "Get *out*!"

The fact that it's pissing Christina off a bit (or a lot) only fuels our giggle-fit. Joy and I continue to cheer, laughing loudly, line kicking our way out of the room.

From behind us, comes the queen's admonition. "CLOSE THE FUCKING DOOR."

"Oh, we've gone and done it now," Joy says and laughs even harder. "I haven't heard her use that much volume in a long while."

"Maybe it'll help her. I just had my cleanse. Time for hers." And I realize it's true, I feel cleansed. Complete.

Sometimes the best thing for a bleeding heart isn't a

band aid, but rather a bit of warm-hearted silliness and whole-hearted laughter.

∽

When I return to my room, I find a present from Joy, obviously placed there while I was with Christina.

Joy had overheard me admire a shoulder bag a friend had purchased from a local tradesman the week prior. I found the bag quite appealing, authentic and classy, nothing *tourista* about it. A good size. Its primary color was a cerulean blue and wouldn't go with a thing I own.

"That is really pretty," I had remarked. "Did he have one in black?"

"Yeah, I think so," she had replied.

Now, there on my bed is the same bag in black. Joy filed that casual remark away and found the time and money to go buy it for me. Joy, a gypsy jewel of generosity. She has scribbled a note onto a piece of standard photocopy paper, folded it, and tucked it inside the bag.

Remember, it reads in big red letters, *you are loved*.

32

THE LAST MORNING

G ary has offered me a ride to the airport today. He is picking his wife up at the same time my flight is scheduled to depart, a fortuitous coincidence eliminating the need for a taxi. My bag is packed, zipped, and sitting outside my door, ready for Toto to carry down the Stair Monster and over to Gary's car. I have only a few things left to do. I feel relaxed. I am an experienced traveler and expert packer. I leave nothing until the last minute, having left too many items in too many hotel rooms over too many decades. I hate rushing and loathe leaving things behind. And today, I must leave Christina behind. I certainly don't want to rush that.

I head up the stairs to get a coffee at 8:00 a.m. The dogs are outside in the garden and Christina's door stands open. I walk right in.

"Morning!" I chirp. "How are you doing?"

"Okay. I had a bit better night." The new medication is working.

"Good. It's picture day. I want a picture, dammit!" I smile, but Christina doesn't. I have mentioned I want a

picture with her before I go at least five times. I suspect
we're both avoiding the finality it will declare.

"I know, I know. After my shower."

"Right. It can be quick. Just one picture. You need
anything? I'm headed upstairs for some coffee."

"No, I'm good. Joy's making me a protein shake." As
if on cue, I hear the blender burst into song upstairs.

"Okay. I'm all packed—"

"Of course you are." Christina smiles.

"I'll be back and forth, hanging out in the garden. I'll
check in later."

After showering and getting dressed in my travel
clothes, I return upstairs for a fresh cup of coffee, then
peek around Christina's door.

"Hey."

"What?" Christina is staring at her open laptop,
concentrating. Her eyes don't leave the screen.

"What are you doing?"

"Amauri is coming in five minutes. I have to get this
list ready for him." She says this with a subtext of 'don't
bother me right now.' She and Amauri, a wonderful high
school student she took under her wing and who adores
her, have been straightening out a bit of a financial
record-keeping mix-up regarding the scholarship
program Christina began for the local school children
years ago. There are over thirty students now provided a
high school and college education through the *Becas*
Program. Christina is transferring her direction and care
of the program over to others. It's been a multi-month
endeavor. This last chore, a dangling thread, will tie off
the hand-off.

"Right. Good. Okay. See you later."

She turns and smiles at me then. "Thanks." The value
of old friends includes understanding.

"As you were," I say and twirl away. I feel remarkably happy and upbeat for a day such as this. Maybe last night's deluge washed the fear and grief away.

As I round the corner of the foyer and exit through the front door to walk back to my room, I see an elderly couple coming up the stairs. Turns out they're only a few years older than me, but physically appear much older. It's something around the eyes, the slope of the shoulders. My mother always says, *Stand up straight and walk with a purpose; you'll look years younger.*

They stop at the top of the stairs, clutching the handrail, and take a few breaths. I move towards them.

"Hi. Can I help you?"

"Hi. We're looking for Christina." The gentleman extends his hand. "The name's Saul. This is my wife, Ruby." He is tall, perhaps six-foot-two, but his shoulders droop. His head holds a few sparse strands of white hair. He wears a striped, cotton knit shirt, the kind that would feel at home on a golf course. His belly strains against his shirt. I can see the outline of his bellybutton. He would be well served to go up a shirt size.

"Hi. Welcome. I'm Cynthia, a friend of Christina's."

"Oh, hello!" the woman says to me. We shake hands. She has carefully coiffed short blond hair, but hair with too much volume and lift to it, like the kind they grow in Texas. She wears a coordinated outfit and too much makeup for this heat. She has a heavy bosom and bottom.

"Is she available?" she asks. Ruby's hands flutter from her sides and come together at her waist.

"Let me check," I respond. "Did you call? Does she know you're coming? Her energy is limited these days, you know." *Guardian to the end.*

"Yes, we know," Saul says somberly. "That's why we're here."

Ruby wrings her hands. "Oh, it's just horrible, horrible. *So* sad. I feel *so* bad for her. *Such* a wonderful woman. She's been *so* kind to us. Ever since we bought here. She was *so* helpful."

She reminds me of a bird whose head twists every which way, constantly startled by life. She twitters her apology for not having called Christina and offers at least three reasons why they didn't, or couldn't, or why it has to be *now*, that they're leaving Boca and just *have* to see Christina, that they have something *important* to tell her.

Her earnest insistence moves me to ask them to wait a moment. I enter the house, closing the front door behind me. I check with Christina and give her their names. She's wrapping up the list for Amauri, looking forward to a shower. I'm leaving in a couple hours. I can tell she's used half her available energy for the day already.

"Oh, man." She sighs and closes her eyes. Her head drops back onto her pillows briefly and then she raises it, and reopens her eyes. "Okay. Give me two minutes. I am so close to being done. I want to wrap this up." She returns her focus to her laptop. "Two minutes."

Two minutes later I lead them inside. They head to Christina's room, almost on tiptoe. I head upstairs and refill my mug.

When I come back down the stairs and pass by Christina's open bedroom door, I see the couple standing next to her bed, leaning from their waists toward her, over the edge of the bed. It looks invasive and feels desperate, somehow. Neither has taken a seat; it appears it will be a short visit. *Good*. I catch a bit of the conversation in passing ". . . and she died only three years ago! This one has levelled us . . ." *Uh, oh*. They're sharing a story of loss and death and pain. On my last morning with Christina. This is going to suck her energy dry. I decide to keep an eye on this.

I return to my room for a final visual sweep. Maya has followed me down the stairs. This is not an uncommon occurrence for her to stop by—I leave my door open most of the day—even Bruja will lounge on my bed some days when the sun streams through the veranda doors and bathes the bed in the warm morning light. But what *is* unusual is a visit from Bella, who *never* comes into my room. Even more unusual is a visit from all three, on the same day, at the same time. It has never happened before.

They all come by as I stuff the last few things in my new handbag and organize its contents for my flight home. I talk pretty to the animals while I putz around and straighten my room.

"Wow. What a surprise! All of you here to say goodbye? That's so nice. I appreciate that."

And then, later, stopping and looking at them all looking at me, "I don't want to go, you know. I don't. I thought about staying, I did, staying until she's gone. But I have stuff to do back home, and it could take a month, and . . . it's time to go, even if I don't want to. It's time. Joy will be here. And I'll be back."

I make my bed, even though I know Isabel will soon strip it and change the sheets. I make my bed in hotel rooms, too. I read somewhere—some army general or someone like that said it—that making your bed in the morning is a good way of setting the tone for the day.

Bruja appreciates my unnecessary efforts and climbs up on my perfectly smooth bedspread. Seems all that practice smoothing Christina's bedspread has paid off. Bruja lays there, just looking at me. She's a beautiful cat and for a brief moment I wonder if I should adopt her. But I'm too mobile at this stage of my life for a pet. There are too many planes, trains and automobiles for animal companionship.

Bella jumps up on the bed. She and Bruja share Christina's bed and are used to each other. Bruja gives Bella a heavy-lidded look of dismissal, and then turns away. Bella wiggles her body and stretches out, watching my face, all wide-eyed expectation. With my bag organizing finished, I sit down on the bed. Maya sits down at my feet and places her head on my knee.

"I'm leaving," I tell them. As if they didn't know. They know. Animals know. My throat tightens.

"Not sure if I'll see you guys again. Take care of our lady, alright?"

I pat Maya's head with my left hand. My right alternatively strokes Bella and Bruja's. They are the proxy for my final goodbye, the last look at my best friend's face. A dress rehearsal. Tears spring to my eyes as I sit there in silence, feeling their warm, soft fur. Seems I am not yet ready for opening night.

Ah, the joy of touch! The physical senses, the ones Christina will leave behind. The ones we take for granted. The ones that both delight and dismay. The ones to be found only in physical form: the taste, texture, and temperature of a favorite ice cream; the feel of warm fur, or the softness of a baby's skin; the sight of a loved one's face or the sound of their voice; the scent of summer jasmine in the breeze or banana bread baking. Such is the seductive sensuality of the senses.

And then there's the pain of them. Life is not a zero-sum game. It's an experience with two halves, like a popsicle. Happiness and sorrow, victory and defeat, shame and pride, you don't get to choose which feelings are okay and which ones you'll deny entry. They all *come with*, like Mattie came with my old place next door, or Bruja comes with this place now. To deny one's pain, to push it away, means to deny also, though unwittingly, one's joy. Both are important evidence of our existence, our shared humanity.

~

I have checked three times. Saul and Ruby are still here. Up and down the stairs I've traipsed. I've stuck my head around the corner of the foyer where I can see them both, still standing there, bedside, still leaning in, still talking. Ruby does most of the talking. A torrent of words fall from her mouth, tumbleweeds loosed to the wind, words so needy they obliterate any awareness of their effect on the listener.

I glance at my watch. 10:28. *That's enough.* It's been an hour. An hour of *my* time. I march upstairs again and into the room.

"Hi." I glance at Christina then Ruby and Saul. "I don't mean to interrupt, but I'm going to." I smile. It is always best to smile in the presence of strangers while wielding a scalpel. "This is our last morning together. I leave for the airport in a little over an hour. And my friend wants to shower. I'm sure you understand." I smile.

Ruby startles. Her eyes widen and she begins apologizing. They hug Christina goodbye and I usher them out, closing her bedroom door behind us. Joy glides down the stairs—she had obviously been waiting for their departure—and quietly slips in right behind us. It's shower time.

Halfway to the front door, and wanting only to be polite, I say, "I overheard some of your conversation. I'm very sorry for your loss. Was it someone close to you?" That stops their forward momentum.

"Our son-in-law." She replies. "He died in March. Shot himself." Ruby's eyes refill with tears and her hands twist the moist Kleenex she holds. "And this after his son committed suicide three years ago! Oh, it's been horrible, just horrible. I don't know what we're going to do." She shakes her head and looks down at the floor. Saul's shoulders stiffen with stoicism. I imagine he has listened to Ruby for so many years that he has become inured to her pain; he carries enough of his own.

"I'm sure it's been a difficult time. You must be devastated," I say sympathetically.

"We are, we are," Ruby answers. "It's, it's . . . *horrible*. And I just *had* to let Christina know. She was so helpful when we first visited Boca, before we bought our place." Ruby glances up at her husband briefly. Saul stares at some distant point out the veranda doors behind me. "And now we need to sell it. We need to go take care of our baby, Myra." She dabs her eyes and works the tissue in her hand.

She tells me that they have two daughters, Sara and Myra. Or had. Sara died of cancer three years ago. Myra's son, their grandson, committed suicide a year later, at age twenty, for reasons they can't understand, that make no sense. And then Myra's husband committed suicide in April, less than a year ago. He called to tell his wife, "I love you, but I can't take it anymore." Then he shot himself. This is the story they have poured forth at Christina's bedside for the past hour in excruciating detail.

Some people's stories will crack your heart in two.

Ruby and Saul are frantic with worry for their remaining daughter who has become catatonic in her grief. All I can do is listen and shake my head and furrow my brow. It's a heart-wrenching story of loss, human loss, and especially family loss. Pain travels through family systems, permeates genealogies, as certainly and insidiously as cancer travels through the body, its poisonous tendrils choking life from its physical host. There are different kinds of death. Some just leave you still breathing.

We say a warm goodbye, the kind you say to strangers you'll most likely never see again. They turn and walk out the front door. For a moment they are framed in the large, oval-shaped oak doorway, in silhouette, his right hand in the small of her back, his wife of forty-eight years. I suspect he knows that spot on her back as well as he knows his own hand. The doorjamb acts as an elegant frame as they step from the shadow of the interior to the blinding light outside. *Snap*. From behind, they form a perfectly framed picture of agony, an outline of an anonymous couple with bent bodies and broken spirits broadcasting desperate sadness, loss, and confusion.

We all know that place of pain. It's where we meet in our humanness.

I pray they find peace.

33

THE FINAL GOODBYE

Christina is out of the shower and dressed for the day. I stride right into her bedroom.

"Okay, lady. It's time. I've got to go."

Christina is propped up on her freshly straightened bedspread, and she is freshly spruced after the shower. Her hair has been dried and styled a bit, and she has a touch of lip gloss on, a nod to our forthcoming—and long awaited—photo op.

"Let's take this fucking picture," she says through gritted teeth. Saul and Ruby's visit has left her utterly drained. She starts to lift herself up from the bed and grimaces. It's the pain, not me, and I know that. And also, the goodbye. I can feel that, too. It's like watching the doctor lift a big-ass needle while saying, "Now, this may hurt a little. Are you ready?" *Fuck no, I'm not ready!*

"Hell, no. Don't move." I wave her initial effort aside. "You stay put. I'm coming in."

"Oh, thank you!" She exhales audibly and falls back onto the pillows.

I climb over her onto the bed, careful to avoid applying any pressure to her frail frame, and position myself in the middle of her queen-size bed on the right side of the queen herself. We tilt our heads together and hold hands. Joy stands at the foot of the bed with my iPhone.

"Okay. Smile. C'mon. Smile!" Joy barks.

But my face has melted, melted like a child trying to hang on to her carefully crafted snowball while warming herself in front of a roaring fire. I cannot smile. I cannot smile. I have been strong all morning, thinking last night was enough, was the end, was a period. But it wasn't, it wasn't, it was only a comma, and my face has fallen off.

"Smile, dammit," Joy admonishes me.

But I can't smile, my smile muscles won't work. They have gone dormant, immobile. The pain has flooded me, like a levy bursting, explosively, the impending physical separation thrusting me underwater. I turn my head to the left and kiss the side of Christina's head.

"Awww . . ." she says and smiles.

"I love you, Christina," I whisper in her right ear.

"I love you, too," she says to the camera.

Snap. Joy captures the moment, that *exact* five second exchange: two sucky, face-melting pictures, and one of me, face buried in Christina's hair, kissing the right side of her head. My face is completely obscured, a side-note to her beatific one. Her face glows. It sums up an entire lifetime and one friendship within it.

"Oh, well, would you look at that!" Joy says. "It's eleven minutes after eleven."

"*Wha-a-t?*" I say, stunned. I hold out my hand for my cell.

"See? Time stamp. Eleven, eleven." *Time!* She hands me the phone and chirps a familiar refrain. "What are you grateful for?" She moves away and reaches for Christina's phone on the bedside table, a little love warrior on the move, completing tasks while giving thanks.

In esoteric sciences like the study of sacred numbers and vibrational medicine, 11:11 holds a high place, some might say the highest place of all. It is not an uncommon thing to notice the same sequence of numbers repeatedly. Some posit that it might be one way angels, or spirit guides, or whatever, communicate with us. Almost daily I seem to look up from whatever I'm doing and notice that my watch or phone or laptop or digital clock reflects some particular sequence. Years ago, for a period of time, it was 1-2-3-4, and I remember a period of noticing 3-3-3, but for the past two years it's been 11:11 and 1:11. Almost every single day, to the point that it's a joke because it will happen in odd places, like a clock on the grocery store wall while I wait in line, or the info boards in the subway station. I look up and there it is, 11:11. And each time, I say a silent *thank you* for something, anything. I take a minute to feel grateful. I didn't make this 11:11 gratitude thing up; it's a real thing lots of people do. Well, some of the people I know.

So, when Joy makes note of the time, announces it, I'm rather blown away, but not really that surprised, more like, *of course it's 11:11*, since I already had a daily routine of taking time out to notice and give thanks. And because it's my existing practice—to notice and reflect and give gratitude on the one's—I was able, in this most precious moment, to recognize and receive an incredible gift from the Universe, a moment of supreme completion and utter gratitude. For me, it reflects the ultimate confirmation of an ongoing conversation.

The 11:11 picture is perfect. It's not about me, it's about Christina, and life, and love, with all of it reflected in her eyes. I'm finally able to smile.

The moment ends and I crab crawl my way off the

foot of her bed. Moments later Toto arrives to carry my bag across the river for me. It's time to leave. I grab my shoulder bag, the one Joy gave me, and lean down for one final physical embrace.

"You're gonna get the merry Meryl life review, I just know it," I say to her neck.

"I'm having it now," she whispers to mine.

We break the embrace. I straighten and look down at my dear friend's face for the very last time. I can no longer stem the tears. My face is melting again and it's time to go; Toto says Gary's waiting for me at the bottom of the stairs.

"Love you, sistah," I choke out. "Save me a seat."

34

WELCOME HOME

After hugging Joy and Isabel goodbye at the front door, I weep my way down the now endearingly endless steps. I see Gary at the bottom well before I get to him. Stopping midway at the pumphouse to wipe my eyes and nose, I gather myself before proceeding the rest of the way down. Gary can tell by my face I've been crying, that I'm still crying behind my sunglasses. He knows. The town knows. I muster a small smile and lift my right hand weakly. "Talk later," I say as I walk by.

I keep moving, past him, aware he cannot keep up, past the ramshackle homes along the path, and the barking dogs behind the gates, and the clucking chickens in the underbrush, past the small *Hotel Pasado*, and toward the bridge. If I keep moving, I might outrun the grief that grips my heart, the finality of this goodbye squeezing truth from my soul and tears from my eyes. I will never see Christina again in the flesh in this lifetime. The next one feels too long a wait.

Once at the bridge, I am well ahead of Gary and Toto, so I stop midway across and look back. Just once, I tell myself, just for a second. *One more video, CC.* I know

I won't see her, or she me, but there is some sort of finish in that final backwards look and my tears begin to lessen. By the time I reach the road, the hand of goodbye has released its grip on my heart and the ache has become less acute.

There is nothing I can do but move forward.

Gary rides in the front passenger seat. A friend drives. There are two stops along the way and snippets of conversation sandwiched between bumps in the road. We talk in fits and starts with extended silences between. Gary is a gentle giant who has lost friends and family to cancer. He shares his stories. It is the way of human connection, that when someone experiences loss, we share our own stories as a way to relate, to comfort, to connect. We do not resent people in pain, but we will often envy people's good fortune or joy. Why them and not us?

But tragedy seems to unite us. In pain, we empathize, individually and collectively. Whether it's the sudden loss of a child that unites a family, the wrath of Mother Nature that unites a community, or the loss of a historical cathedral that unites the world, pain, loss and grief are the very reasons for unification because they are so universally shared, and hence, understood. Pain is the bass line in the symphony of the human experience, the drumbeat keeping time with joy's melody.

The human story is a tapestry of commonality, one thread interlocked with another, intricately and irrevocably woven together, shards of shrapnel to the heart, transformed into pearls and precious stones. And then, individually, added to the corner of the tapestry we are privileged to weave.

Wisdom will make master weavers of us all, if we let Her.

I get checked in and through security, find an open spot on the standard issue airport seats, plop myself down, and settle in to wait for my flight. Before I can access the Kindle in my shoulder bag, a man sits down next to me on my right. He is a very large man. Football large. He is a super-size version of the average man. Maybe mid to late fifties, he has grey hair cropped short. He has an air of military about him. Glancing over his left shoulder at me, he catches me glancing at him and grins sheepishly. "I take up a lot of room," he says, "but I make up for it by being a nice guy."

I smile in return, also sheepish at having been caught looking at him. It appears he's used to it.

"No worries," I say. I move my bag from beside me to under my legs in order to give him more room. As he adjusts his bags around his own legs, I see something flash on his huge right hand, a very large flash from his larger hand. Pretending not to look—and hoping not to get caught this time—I wait for the source to be revealed.

It's a ring. It's a super-size ring for a super-size guy, a Super Bowl ring. "Is that a Super Bowl ring?" I ask. I bet he's never heard that one before.

I've never seen a Super Bowl ring in person before. They are *huge*. And they're heavy. I know this because he takes it off to let me hold it. It has a big honking diamond in the center, and I can fit two fingers through its opening. He tells me he played professional football back in the day and won a ring as a Dallas offensive lineman in the '70s. It turns out he's from Regina. (That's in the

Canadian Prairies.) You don't meet many of those folks out and about. How many people from Regina have you met in an airport that isn't located in Regina? He's on his way to a meeting in Toronto. We begin trading stories the way strangers in airports sometimes do.

We've twisted toward each other, enjoying our conversation. He's a warm and engaging storyteller. I listen. Then he asks me about my story. What brought me to Boca? I tell him about Christina, and he tells me about his brother-in-law who died of bladder cancer not too long ago. When he speaks of it, the pain of the loss is evident, if only briefly. *"A heart that is broken is a heart that is open."* We meet on the bridge of universal pain—loss—and acknowledge the shared experience.

An announcement comes over the intercom. "Oh, that's me." His flight is boarding. He begins to gather his stuff.

"It was very nice to meet you," I say. "Safe travels."

He rises from his seat with a practiced push off, turns, and looks down at me. "It was nice to meet you, too." He extends his beefy right hand, the one with the ring, and looks at me kindly, another gentle giant. "I hope your friend passes peacefully," he says. I believe him. He's not simply being polite, he means it.

"Me, too," I reply. "That's all I'm praying for now."

My plane lands in Toronto on time and, after customs, in a matter of an hour I've trained my way through various stops to Union Station in the center of the city. It's frigid cold outside and my heavy sweater is no match for the whipping wind, so I grab a taxi out front for the six-block ride to my downtown apartment. We pass a convenience store on the way and I ask the driver to pull over while I run inside for some fresh milk for my coffee in the morning. I grab some ice cream, too, because, well, because I want it. Small pleasures.

The cab arrives at my entrance and I climb the front steps with my small, expertly packed bag in one hand and my new shoulder bag from Joy in the other. I wait the normal amount of time for an elevator. I traipse my way down the hallway to my front door, insert the key, and step inside. I drop my bags, shuck off my coat, and hang it on the hook to the right of the door. I walk into the kitchen and flip on the light switch.

And stop dead in my tracks.

I mention all the little steps involved in getting home because the time involved in each is variable depending on, for example, the flight and weather interference, or the length of the line at customs, or the wait for the next train, or red lights on downtown streets, or the speed or lack thereof of the little old man who owns the convenience store as he operates his new computer system. All these things take time, time that adds up.

OMG. Time!

So, imagine my utter amazement when I flip on the light in the kitchen and it reveals the digital oven clock reflecting the time, shouting the exact minute I walk through the door. And why my delight? Yep, you guessed it. 11:11. I burst out laughing, almost dropping the milk. In hindsight, I should have taken a picture, because, I mean, *really*? 11:11 a.m. The goodbye picture: 11:11 p.m. Hello and welcome home!

There are 1440 minutes in a day. (I had to Google that—I want to make a point, and for some people numbers help make grey things easier to grasp.) That means that there are exactly *two* chances out of 1440 to see that sequence of numbers on any given day. That's a .07 percent chance (I had to Google that, too.), which is way less than 1 percent, which are really, really, lousy odds. (I knew that all by myself.) But to hit the same sequence, twice, in a memorable, noticeable, confirmable way? On a day like this? The odds are astronomical and beyond my ability to even begin to ask Google to calculate.

The point is, it's only a coincidence if I think it is. Which is one way to look at it. Another is that it isn't, that it is the Universe talking to me, communicating, continuing the conversation. It doesn't matter which view you choose; meaning is made by which one you use.

What a wonderful, fulfilling Friday, my fourth and final Friday with my friend, I think as I put the milk in the refrigerator. I said goodbye to my best friend in the morning and now I get to eat Haagen Dazs coffee ice cream exactly twelve hours later and two countries away.

And the Universe traveled with me, and just wanted me to know.

35

THE COUNTDOWN SPEEDS UP

Saturday: January 26, 2019

The next morning, it's icy cold. There is a foot of new snow on the ground. It is a winter white landscape with whistling winds. I trudge my way through it, my limp laptop bundled in my arms, and am one of the first in line waiting for the Apple store to open at the Eaton Centre, in downtown Toronto. I mill around with the masses, awaiting my turn at the Genius Bar. I am not sure that's the name they should use. In any case, after a technician in the back checks out my woefully non-functioning laptop, it is determined that not only does it require a new keyboard, it also needs a new I/O port—whatever that is—and so we're looking at a minimum of $900 and at least another week without my laptop. The very notion of additional downtime sets my heart aflutter, and not in a good way. *I have shit to do.*

I take the path of least resistance. I buy a new laptop.

Sunday: January 27, 2019

WhatsApp with Joy:

Me: *How's our girl today?*

Joy: *Not great. Started new meds yesterday and that did not go well. Doctor's coming back today to give her meds and fluids through IV.*

Me: *Shit. Happening fast. Sending love to you and Momma C.*

Joy: *Feeling your love.*

~

"Hey! How are you? How was your trip?"

Kim has called to catch up. We've been friends since the mid-nineties. The middle child of three girls, and a single mom to one grown son, Kim is one of my few precious first level friendships.

"Oh, Kimmie, it was great, just great, a really special experience. I haven't really digested it all yet. It's hard to believe I was with her two days ago." I glance out the window across from me. It's snowing. Again. But it's Sunday and I don't have to go out into it, so it's okay. I quite enjoy watching snow from within four warm walls. "There's lots to tell you, but too much for this conversation. Let's wait until we get together."

"Sounds good. Just give me the highlights. How's she doing?"

"Not good. The pain's increasing. It won't be long."

Kim's parents died within weeks of each other during the summer of 2013. Both had cancer, though different forms, and both hung on for the other person, outliving their doctors' estimates. They had been married over fifty years and were devoted to each other. Her dad had been an ophthalmologist, her mom—as was the societal norm of the day—managed the home and raised the children. Kim spent three years between their diagnosis and death in a state of perpetual dread. When the first finally succumbed to the disease and left for whatever comes after, the other followed within weeks. It was a severe summer of loss for my friend. It was also the summer of my broken knee and so I had been sidelined from the immediacy of her experience; I was physically incapable of being there with my friend at her parents' funerals. It was a hard and lonely time for her and her sisters, both of whom still lived in their childhood hometown of Ottawa. Kim, though, lives in Toronto, and she felt the emotional distance on a physical level, especially the loss of her role as a daughter. It died along with her parents. She is a sister and mother now.

Kim's a single mom. Her son is grown and gone, but she fought being single for decades, devastated by her divorce, determined to find someone with whom she would feel whole. It was not so much the loss of her husband, the *man,* that she regretted, but rather the role of *wife* that stormed out with him. That role carried with it a certain social acceptance and a sort of ease, invitations to dinner parties and the like. Now, hosts were required to ensure another single to balance the table, odd numbers being uncomfortable. She had to learn to walk into events alone—as have I—and hang her own coat, get her own drink, seek her own seat, create her own connections. She's done a fabulous job.

Kim and I share that aspect of our existence, being on our own, though she would welcome the opportunity to have a partner and I declared myself done a decade ago. *Done.* Two husbands is enough, at least for me, though my worldly CEO brother assures me that it takes at least *three* husbands before billionaires will consider you marriage material, which seems counterintuitive to

me, but then I'm not as worldly, wise, or sophisticated as
he is. Or, maybe he was just joking. In either case, I have
no need nor desire for a relationship of the romantic sort.
People say, "Yes, but what about companionship? Don't
you get lonely?" And the short answer is no, I don't get
lonely. Not on my own. I quite like my own company.
The loneliest I've ever felt was always in the company of
another. You can feel utterly alone in the midst of a
crowd, and you can feel completely connected all by
yourself. It helps, though, to believe you're *not* alone even
when you *appear* alone. Angels and such. And also,
quantum physics.

"It's so hard saying goodbye, isn't? It's the hardest
thing I've ever done, saying goodbye to them," Kim remi-
nisces. "Mom waited until we left the room before taking
her last breath. She wanted to spare us that."

I remember now that she had told me of that gesture
by her mother. Her mom had been a woman of steely
strength who supported her husband through medical
school. Whether by choice or chance, she went to her
death the same way she carried herself in life, with stoic
determination and maternal devotion.

Kim and I talk on and my mind wanders a bit,
fingering the hem of a thought, the paradox of feeling
alive in the midst of death. Kim's dearest friend, her
fifteen-year-old Wheaton Terrier, is slowly wasting away,
and watching his decline is as painful to Kim as watching
Christina has been for me. I tune back into the
conversation.

"Why does it take watching someone else die to wake
us to the wonders of being alive?" she says. "The small,
daily wonders." Kim stops suddenly. "Damn! I just
stepped in *poop*!"

How do you step in poop inside? Was she talking to
me from outside? It didn't sound like it, as there were no

outside background noises, but maybe she was walking Carter in a quiet park somewhere. But in this snow? That was hard to believe; it had been coming down hard for several hours.

"Where are you?" I ask.

"In my *house*!" She's annoyed. Well, at least my background radar-reading skills are still accurate. "It's Carter. His hips won't support him, won't let him move when he's on the wood floor. They just slide out from under him and he just lays there if I'm not around to pick him up. I don't know why he insists on laying on the floor instead of his bed." She takes a breath. She's walking around, getting something to pick up the poop.

"Maybe he gets hot, and the floor cools him down," I insert in the pause. "He wears a fur coat all the time, you know?" I have a knack for obvious observations, extraneous and unnecessary. Like a seat filler at an awards show, I keep the conversation moving. Or perhaps it's the cliché of the old lady who lives alone and talks to herself, maybe that's why I don't get lonely.

Kim continues. "I know, but *really*. It's on my new boots! *Damn*."

She's walking around, I can tell. I can hear the *click clack* of her boots on the creaking hardwood floor when she steps off the carpeted areas of her home. As I said, I have excellent background radar-reading skills.

"And it's on the *carpet*. *Dammit* Carter!" Kim starts talking to her beloved companion. "Come on, let's go. Outside. Now. Let's go." Her tone belies the devoted care she's provided him and the enormous love they share. His impending death will leave her partnerless again.

She's bending over (I can tell), coaxing him along, one hand on his hindquarters. They are moving toward the door. It's a slow process. I hear her front door open and the sound of Carter's toenails scratching as he scrambles down the stone steps toward the yard.

I remember when Megan, my chocolate Labrador retriever who died in 1999, could no longer support herself and I would come downstairs in the morning to find her still laying on her bed, large nuggets near her tail. She was thirteen and unable to lift herself any longer. She also couldn't control her bowels. Her tail would wag but she wouldn't lift her head from her bed, and her eyes wouldn't meet mine. Happiness and shame were at war inside her. Dogs know guilt. They express shame. They just don't carry those feelings in a suitcase when they travel to their tomorrows, as we humans do, unpacking each carefully folded accessory and giving it space in our new locale. But dogs feel it in the moment and they know when they've fallen short.

It's excruciating to watch your beloved family member — human or canine — become enfeebled, to witness the life force energy drain from their physical bodies, to feel the fading. But inherent to living are the practical aspects of death: who to contact, where and when to honor, how to move on through our grief. We will avoid these conversations with our aged loved ones, thinking that it is somehow morbid, but it is not. Death walks with us, hand in hand, every day. It is fundamental and necessary. Thoughts of end-stage decision making linger in the periphery of daily living for those who understand this. Perhaps this is one reason why people who have had a near-death experience often become more passionate about their lives as a result of almost losing them. Awareness of death's companionship releases us from fear of its eventual arrival. It's already here! We know that about our pets while we love them, that they'll most likely die before us and we will cry and miss them. Why do we forget that with people?

It seems a paradox to me that we are oftentimes more compassionate with our animals at the end of life than we are with ourselves or our family and friends. Why is euthanasia okay for a dog but not for a person? That old adage—dog is God spelled backwards—might be bang on. I wonder, now, if it may be our primary purpose on this planet, as a species, to learn to love ourselves, and by implication others, like we love our pets, to show each other the same compassion we do a dying dog. We might just save the planet if we do.

The conversation begins to wind down. She's watching her dog in the yard through the beveled glass window of her front door, hoping he'll rid himself of whatever additional poop he might still hold, and itching to clean what he has already gifted her inside. We make plans to see each other soon.

"I've got to go." Kim ends the phone call. "My dog's covered in snow and I'm covered in poop."

Monday: January 28, 2019

Joy: *Hey girl! Doctor couldn't make it yesterday. He's coming tonight with another doctor to put a catheter in for her fluids, and a pic line for food and meds. She's going to shower in a bit, possibly her last . . . say a prayer for our girl today. I'll touch base when I know more.*

Me: *Sending so much love and support. Leo called it during his last visit. He said, 'It'll be fast now.'*

I text her a photo of the freshly fallen snow on my patio table, left overnight by a menopausal Mother Nature. It's not that I hate winter, it's that I hate winter in Toronto. Not so much in Boca, though. Environment may not determine happiness, but it sure does influence it mightily.

Tuesday: January 29, 2019

Joy: *Good morning! The mini surgery in Christina's room last night was successful! Late night for everyone. She's being hydrated and medicated through the IV now. Her breathing is good, and she's been sleeping for about seven hours. She looks good, and peaceful.*

And then, few minutes later:

Joy: *I just read all our messages to Christina and she wants me to tell you she loves you, that this morning is so beautiful, and she asks that you take a moment and feel her love. She says it is a magical and beautiful way to experience the end of life.*

Me: *I can feel it from here. I'm sending my love to you both in return. Glad to hear she's in less pain. Missing you both.*

Joy is the perfect person for Christina right now. Her kitchen release has revived her natural good nature and she is nourishing our friend with love. It is helping to relieve Christina's pain, as well as her own—and mine.

36

WHO NEEDS EARRINGS?

P ain occurs on every level of the human operating system. There is physical pain, and flesh and bone pain. There is emotional pain, the pain of anger, loss, and regret. And there is intellectual pain, when we're stuck on a project or feel isolated and unable to articulate our thoughts and feelings.

I would argue that underlying those three levels is the motherboard, the fundamental spiritual platform on which the other three operating systems depend for proper functioning. When that platform is healthy, the software programs run more smoothly.

An interesting characteristic of the physical software, at least to me, is the fact that human beings cry different types of tears in response to different stimuli. There are three types of tears. There are basal tears, which occur all day long in minor amounts and keep the cornea lubricated. Reflex tears, otherwise known as automatic emergency tears, are a response to onions or tear gas or smoke. And then there are psychic tears, evoked by strong emotions.

Photographer Rose-Lynn Fisher put dried tears under a microscope and discovered that the molecular structure of human tears actually alters depending on the reason for them. We might cry in victimhood or in victory, when we're sad or when we're happy. The structure of tears shed in joy differs from the structure of tears shed in grief. Under a microscope, one can see that the actual *state* of the molecule changes depending on the motivation behind their production. That's more than transformation; that's a new state of being, like boiling water becoming steam.

Is that what happens when we die? Do we simply disappear? Do we transform? Or do we transmute, becoming a different chemical construction? One that obscures us from those still living, those who in physical form are so slowed down in their molecular motion as to be visible to the eye. The eagle and the hummingbird both flap their wings to fly from one place to another, but the latter's wings move so swiftly as to blur into transparency when viewed by the human eye. Is that what happens to us when we step through the veil? Do we go from a larger, slower, more easily viewable state, to one that whisks us away—or that part of us that weighs twenty-one grams and disappears from our body weight at the moment of death—to another, faster moving state of being? A blurred disappearance, a transparent transition.

Given my experience of drowning at not quite four years of age, and the memories I hold of what I can only call a *trip to somewhere*, I am fascinated by these questions. I do believe in the existence of the soul, because my little girl consciousness saw *something* on the other side, experienced a moment of clarity and understanding and unconditional love beyond my ability to adequately articulate it. I saw and felt something that has propelled me to ask these kinds of questions and to pursue answers all my life.

I am reminded of Ranier Maria Rilke's wise advice to a young poet. "Have patience with everything unresolved in your heart," he wrote, "and try to love the questions themselves . . . Do not search for answers, which could not be given to you now, because you would not be able to live them. And the point is to live everything. So, live the questions now. Perhaps, then, someday far in the future, you will gradually, without even noticing it, live your way into the answer."

Maybe that's the point, the whole point of the teeny, tiny, little lives we live. Maybe that's all it's about, to live our way into our own answers, to claw our way to clarity through the mud of mistakes and the quicksand of pain. Maybe the whole point is to carve a purpose from the mountains and the landslides of our life.

When taken as a fragment of the history of mankind, not a single one of us matters that much for that long, not really. Not Churchill or Obama or Gandhi or Mother Teresa or your mom or dad or sister or son. Not even Einstein. And, certainly not you or me. But examined under the microscope, through an individual eye, every life is as precious and important and as unique as the tears we each shed.

Wednesday: January 30, 2019

I finally finish unpacking. It's not high on my list, unpacking, which is weird. It's the opposite to my careful packing process, or morning bed making. I'm quite content to continue walking around the open suitcase in my bedroom. It feels as though by unpacking, by doing

laundry and putting things away, I might somehow dilute
—or displace—the intensity and freshness of the memories marked *forever*. I don't want anything to dissipate the
immediacy of the exquisite experience.

But, it has been five days and there are things in my
suitcase that need to be washed and put away. It is the
dead of winter in Toronto, the ground is covered in ice,
and I've got stinky bathing suits sitting in an open suitcase on the floor. *What's wrong with this picture?* With a
heavy sigh, I grit my teeth and get started. Two piles of
laundry begin to accumulate on the floor—colored and
whites—and another pile on the bed, where I toss the
non-laundry items: hair drier, personal care items, the
Kindle cord, clothes I didn't wear, shoes and sandals I
did wear, and the book I grabbed during Christina's
closet purge.

Once I've thrown a load in the washer and put the
personal care items under the sink, I pick up the book
and inspect it more closely. I had only read the title when
I first chose it, *Conversation: A History of a Declining Art*. I
had intended to begin reading it while still in Boca, but
my last couple of days there held more important priorities. Looking at the book now, I notice that its cover art
consists of hand drawn, brightly feathered birds, five of
them, perched on two rungs of a three-rung bird ladder,
seemingly chirping away at each other. Pretty. Above the
title at the very top is a snippet from a review in small
italic font, *A marvelously clear and vigorous exploration of the
history of conversation*. Hmm, I think, this could be
interesting.

But what I notice next is disappointing. Because, as I
think to myself, *good get on the book, CC*, immediately upon
its heels sounds the slender slice of regret. Christina
didn't give me anything personally before she died. She
had nothing pulled aside just for me. No physical

memento. No earrings. Joy got earrings. All I got was this stupid book. And one that *I* chose, not Christina. And I totally forgot to ask her to inscribe it! *Crap.*

I hadn't thought that selfish, envious thought since sitting on the tarmac, staring out the plane window on the airstrip in Puerto Vallarta while waiting to take off. At that particular moment I felt absolutely okay to be leaving. I felt complete and at peace. So, when the earrings thought popped up, I had been able to whisk it aside with gratitude and the knowledge that I had more. I had an 11:11 picture. That was enough. At least, I thought it was.

So, when the ratty, tatty thought once again sneaks out from its seductive sewer hole, I am briefly saddened all over again. Christina *didn't* give me something and why *not* and that I must still *care* and how fucking *human* and low-level is *that* and *fuck*, now I'm pissed off. I'm disappointed with myself. Because I should be better than this. *Says who?* I'm arguing with myself. So, I stop — always the best way to win — and put down the whip, sit on my bed, hold the book in my hands, sigh, and stare at the cover. Well, I think, I got this stupid book. I guess should read it. I open it and begin.

Books are worshiped in my family. We were raised on reading before the age of computers and video games. We were raised to honor books and the words they contain. Every Christmas, every child would receive one book, carefully chosen by my mother and father. My mother would inscribe each book with her beautiful penmanship, the kind of cursive no longer taught in schools. Consequently, upon opening any book, we were trained to start there, with the inscription. So, I begin on the first page, the blank one, because that's usually where inscriptions are written, or at least, my mother's were.

But the first page is blank. I turn to the next page,

the page before the title page, and find an inscription in elegant cursive. *I thought so.* This is not terribly surprising as almost every book in Christina's library was a donation from someone. But this elegant handwriting is the kind you don't see much these days—cursive—and well executed, like my mother's handwriting, written by someone who had taken time to space the words and make sure the lines were all straight and even. In pale blue ink the inscription reads:

> *For Joseph Michael*
> *From MM*
> *With love,*
> *Christmas 2012*

I read the inscription again. Wait a minute . . . *2012?* I was *at* Case la Ventana for Christmas in 2012, with Christina and Joy, and my sister, Jenny, and her husband, Joe, Joy's brother, and their daughter, and my sons . . . *wha-a-t?* Wait a minute. What *is* this?

I stare at the message, the writing, and recognize both. *Holy smokes.*

This is my *mother's* handwriting! My own mother, whose kids and grandchildren call her MM, because her name is Marcia Mary. *OMG. Another Mary!*

Everything slows down, and, as they say, time stands still. It doesn't compute right away, the pinball has bounced too quickly, moved too far, too fast, and in too many directions, but in a couple of seconds I've put it together: My mother must have sent along some gifts with Jenny and Joe back in 2102, for them to open in Boca on Christmas, and this was one I hadn't seen Joe open. *That* was how it had found its way to Casa la Ventana. Knowing Joe, he had either already read it and left it behind in Christina's lending library for others to enjoy, or knew he never would, so he left it for someone else to pack into a suitcase for the trip home. Someone like me.

This particular book—one of hundreds we went through the day of the great closet purge and the only one I kept—was a gift from my mother to my brother-in-law, my sister's husband of thirty years and Joy's dear brother. It was the only thing I took from Casa la Ventana. What are the odds? Calculate *that*, Google.

Who needs earrings when acknowledgements like this have been prepared for me? Before, I needed to be reminded of my value. Now, I realize I am no less special than Joy because she got earrings, and no more special because I got this book, one with my mother's elegant handwriting preserved inside.

Pain illuminated is pain alleviated.

Thinking I have gotten *the message* I see no reason to turn each page in order. *Transmission received.* I sort of thumb-flip through the pages, ready to move on with my day. A small bookmark falls out. It is a simple design, Times New Roman font in a warm white against a solid navy blue background. It contains a short, simple sentence.

The meaning of life is to live it.

Simple, yet profound. Roger, Captain.

Some days, days like today, moments like this, the only thing I can do is stare. And from the fringes of that stare creep tears, like a chorus that builds, slowly, in unison, after the opening bars of music, after the intro-duction of the theme, the melody, toward a final full-chested, long-held note of completion. I am brought to my spiritual knees in those moments. They are beyond words.

And these tears, these awestruck tears, are filled with gratitude, wonder, and delight. That makes them the opposite of sad tears.

And they're mine, alone, unique, and special.

37

A FRIEND IN NEED

Thursday: January 31, 2019

A text from Sally dings on my phone.

You available tomorrow morning? I have to take Sparkle to the vet for some tests and need some help getting her there.

I've known Sally as long as Kim. She, too, is a first level friend. She is also the reason I live where I live, in her apartment building, a marvelous co-op, on whose overfull wait list I languished for six years before a place finally opened up. I moved in in the spring of 2017, one month before Alan informed me he had cancer, and one year before Christina told me the same thing.

Sally has lived in this building for over twenty years. She has a two bedroom apartment on the fourth floor down the hall from mine. Had Sally not alerted me to an opening on the waitlist, which allowed me the opportunity to get my name on it, I might not have snagged such a remarkable place in downtown Toronto. It's got two bedrooms, two floors, a balcony, trees outside, and—

most important of all—an assigned underground parking spot. Gold. I'm never moving.

Sally carries a dry wit in her hip pocket, with a deadpan delivery I find inordinately amusing. Loyal to a fault, her analytic mind is well suited to serve as the right hand of a rich lawyer, one who is actually a good guy. He represented me in the carbon monoxide case—Sally held my hand the whole way—so I have only positive things to say about this particular rich lawyer boss, and Sally, as well. She has begun to think about what comes afterwards, though, about retirement. How can I say this? Sally's not particularly good with change. It causes her anxiety. A lot of things cause her anxiety: the weather, the world, illness, the unknown. Sally doesn't respond well to uncertainty.

At the top of her priority pole is anything to do with animals. Unmarried, now orphaned, with one distant sister and no children of her own, animals fill that void. She supports various charitable animal related efforts and donates her time to the local SPCA where, after appropriate training, she now gets to cuddle with rabbits on Friday nights. As I've mentioned before, a woman's needs change in her sixties if she's partnerless on purpose. A Friday night date with a bunch of friendly, furry animals that don't jabber at you is an ideal date.

And at the very, very top of Sally's life list, ahead of her sister or her friends, are her animals. Sally is a cat lady. She's had cats, well, forever. She keeps six bowls on the kitchen floor, full of dry food, for two cats. She likes them to have a choice. After the deaths of her previous pets, Grouper and Tank—the passing of which left her immobilized—she fostered, but was unable to risk loving that deeply again, to risk the pain of the inevitable loss. That's the thing about love, the paradox of it. Pain and joy are all wrapped up in the same package.

To those who know her, Sally oozes compassion, to her own detriment, sometimes. Like Leo, she can seem crusty on the outside, but is marshmallow on the inside. Sally has been there for me through some difficult times and is a wonderful friend, so I like to help her out when I can, and have watched her cats on many occasions.

I respond to her text by calling.

"Hey. What's with Sparkle?" Sparkle is one of two white kittens she adopted seven years ago. I went with her the day she picked them up, driving her there and back. Sally doesn't do well with moving vehicles, especially while carrying anxious cats in carriers.

"Oh. Hi." Sally is sad, I can tell. She explains that Sparkle has not been eating and is losing weight. The vet has been unable to diagnose her, and has recommended some additional tests. Sally wants me to drive her to the specialist's office. She's concerned that Sparkle may have cancer.

"Sure. Happy to. When's the appointment?"

"Ten o'clock in the morning."

"Okay. I'll be at your door around nine-fifteen."

Sally pauses. "Maybe we should say nine o'clock. I might have some trouble getting her in the carrier. She hates it."

"Right. Nine. See you then."

There's genuine pain and then there's manufactured pain. The former pays in the present, the latter borrows from tomorrow.

Why is that? Why do we borrow pain? We *all* do it, go out and rent it from tomorrow. We go into the future, pluck a possible outcome, one we *don't* want, bring it back to today, and feel it in the present moment, now. As though by doing so we can somehow both plan for and fend off an unwanted future. How stupid is that?

But then, love renders us all stupid. All of us.

If we're lucky.

~

Thursday evening a text *ding*s.

It's from Christina: *Love you.*

Smiling, I type right back: *Love you, too. Forever.*

Words. Damn, I love words. Wonderful, wonderful words.

38

MOURNING IN THE MORNING

Friday: February 1, 2019, 6:13 a.m.

I wake early for some reason, at 6:00 a.m. I usually wake naturally, somewhere close to 7:00. This is a result of the flexibility of self-employment and no children in the house. I'm sipping my first coffee of the morning when I hear a *ding*. Someone's texting me early. It's from Joy: *She's gone.*

Yesterday's text message was Christina's very last and most precious words to me.

Later, a Facebook post announces it to everyone else:

Hello friends and family, this is Joy. It is with a very heavy heart that Nathan, Karen, and I share with you that our dear, sweet Christina Martell passed away this morning in her home here in Boca de Tomatlán. We held her hands and spoke to her sweetly as she took her last breaths. It was so peaceful and so very graceful, exactly how she wanted it to be. I hope that you all take great comfort in knowing that she is no longer in pain.

Christina was a bright and beautiful light who now shines a path for us to follow.

6:55 a.m.

I process my shock and grief—*one week, she lived only one week more! She texted me yesterday!*—the way I do, by banging it out on my keyboard.

By 8:00 a.m. I have written Christina's eulogy within a blog post.

"In the end, only three things matter: how much you loved, how gently you lived, and how gracefully you let go of the things not meant for you." ~ Buddhist saying

As I mentioned in last week's blog, in which I pondered the nature of paradoxes, I had just returned from visiting my dear friend of over three decades, Christina Martell, in a dusty little fishing village along the Pacific coast of Mexico.

Today, Friday, February 1st, 2019, Christina died, peacefully, and pain-free, in her own bed, with her dogs and her cat and her son and adopted daughter by her side. She chose to leave with dignity and grace and gratitude.

During my visit south, Mary Oliver, the Pulitzer-winning poet who often spoke of the paradox of life within death, died herself. In one of my favorite poems, When Death Comes, *she ponders how she wants to leave the world when her times arrives, wishing to be able to embrace death after having been "married to amazement" her whole life.*

*I'd like to be able to say that when my time comes.
Christina already can.*

*Christina was a remarkable woman, a force of nature
who truly took the world into her arms, and the little
town of Boca under her wings. She created a sanctuary
for countless numbers of people in countless ways over the
years.*

*She began a scholarship program so children could
attend high school. One of the last things we did together
was to go through those financials and ascertain things
were in order.*

*She got a clinic built for the town. For years she wooed
donors and created alliances. She got kids to go to the
dentist. She drove them into Puerto Vallarta herself. She
got the dentist to donate his services. She arranged for
water purifiers, trail-trash pick-up . . . the contributions
she has made to that community are too numerous to
name, her impact on a wide number and variety of individuals too vast to realize.*

*I am reminded that change begins one person at a time,
and we can, indeed are, for better or worse, creating a
ripple effect that we cannot begin to imagine, every
moment of every day.*

*I was fortunate to call her friend but blessed that she
allowed me to call her sister.*

*As I type these words, only hours after her death, in a
vain attempt to both curtail my tears while honoring her
life, messages are arriving from all over the world: the
U.K., Canada, France, the States.*

Christina made a difference in the lives of many people.

It is a paradox that sometimes it takes death to remind us how precious and fleeting life really is.
And I am reminded, once again, viscerally, of how important it is to pay attention. To notice and respond. To honor the dance of death as we waltz with life.

Another paradox: My heart is broken open on the floor and yet full of joy.

The ache of gratitude has elbowed out the pain of loss.

Because another human hero has headed home.

"When your time comes to die, be not like those whose hearts are filled with fear of death, so that when their time comes, they weep and pray for a little more time to live their lives over again in a different way. Sing your death song and die like a hero going home." ~Tecumseh

I can now see that completion cleans wounds like a disinfectant staves off infection. It allows the pain of loss to become that of healing.

With hope on the horizon.

39

PEACE

9:00 a.m.

I knock on Sally's door. She opens it immediately. Her bag sits ready by the door. After a hug and pleasantries, we lure Sparkle from upstairs. I get down on the floor with her and feign affection in order to get her in my lap. I now have her in my grasp. Sally lunges for the closet where hides the evil cat carrier. Sparkle sees it and her body tightens, but it's too late, I've got a firm hold on her. And, in she goes. We'll be plenty early for the appointment.

Sally coos while I drive. She turns over her left shoulder from the front passenger seat every so often and sticks a finger through the cat cage resting on the back seat. She wiggles her finger in Sparkle's face. Sally must think that this is soothing. For her, I guess, it is.

It does not soothe me, however. I'm in mourning. The thing is, though, it doesn't show, and I know that it doesn't show, because my pain is not cathartic. I'm not torn in two, rent apart. Sure, I cried while writing the blog, but I didn't sob. I *feel* the loss, of course I do, but my pain is not borrowed or stolen, it is not an explosive force, like a shrapnel bomb shredding its victim to bits. It is a welcome visitor, no longer anticipated, but arrived, here, now.

And, so, I sit at the wheel of my car, next to another friend full of fear and pain who is unaware of my own yet. It's not as though I'm forcing back tears. It's not that. It's that I don't feel the need to cry them, now, here, with Sally, or to even share the news. It's too personal, too fresh, too mine.

Sally keeps cooing. I listen and respond with one ear while the other is glued to another station broadcasting from another place, another planet. I smile often and my smiles are not forced, but real, and, in fact, I feel oddly calm despite the knowledge that Christina no longer breathes. Her spacesuit is empty, she has stepped out of it, and I am left to travel on this spaceship Earth without her. And in the company—on *this* morning, of *all* mornings—with another friend who doesn't believe that she, too, wears a space suit.

Sally holds no spiritual beliefs. The notion of God is too amorphous; it makes her anxious. In an uncertain landscape, *that* planet, the Spirituality Planet, is full of unknowns, full of greys. It is a planet with which I am familiar. I visit often. I trust it. Sally doesn't. For over two decades I have conducted a five-day spiritual retreat. Sally has not yet attended. The irony is not lost on me.

We find a parking place and wind our way around piles of snow, carefully carrying the cat carrier. Sally continues to coo. Sparkle stays quiet inside. Maybe it's working. I scurry ahead and hold the front door open. We sit and wait. The technician comes for Sparkle at 10:30. There have been a couple of emergencies and they're a bit backed up already. Sally and the cage follow her down the hall and into a room. I sit and think about Christina.

After the post-examination debrief with the doctor, in which Sally has requested my presence, and all the *what if* questions, and more tears and tissue, Sally's eyes are swollen, and her voice is small and high pitched. She's scared. To her, this is her child, her family. The doctor has no answers yet, only suggestions, guesses, and reassurances.

"Why don't we wait and see what the tests show. We'll know more then."

"And you'll call me, right? With the results?"

"I'll call you as soon as I get them."

"How long?"

"It'll take a couple of days. Since it's Friday, I doubt I'd hear anything until Tuesday."

"And if it's cancer?"

"Let's just wait for the results. Go home and enjoy your weekend. Play with Sparkle."

And on it went. Circular thought patterns, repetitious questions, a desperate search for the salve of some sort of certainty in the midst of confusion and impending imaginary loss. But after fifteen minutes, Sally finds none. There is no new news, hence Sparkle still has cancer in Sally's mind.

Whoever that doctor is, she gets a gold star for patience. I bet she's practiced it often. She's good at it.

Once we're back in the car and on the way home, I finally tell Sally about Christina.

"So, my friend died." Me and that scalpel again. "Christina. The one I was visiting in Mexico." I pause. Sally whips her head around toward me.

"Oh, I'm so sorry! When did she pass?"

"This morning," I say evenly. "At 6:13." I keep my

eyes on the road in front of me. I know how Sally will respond.

And she does. "Why didn't you *tell* me? You didn't need to drive me. I could've canceled the appointment, moved it." Sally goes straight to guilt. Anxious people often do that. "I feel horrible," she concludes, looking down at her lap. In the pinball machine of life, Sally does not believe in using the flippers. It's one of her most endearing traits.

"Aren't you *sad*?"

I turn to look at her and smile. "It's okay, Sal. I'm okay. Sparkle is not. I don't mind doing this, not at all." I've had hours of soothing cooing and plastic chair waiting time in which to think, and feel, and sort. "In fact, it's been a rich experience," I say. "This whole morning. I'm glad to do it." The light turns green and I face forward again.

"You must be heartbroken."

Yes, I think, I must. I *should*, but that implies a brokenness, and I do not feel broken. On the contrary, I feel whatever is the opposite of that. Unbroken? No, just not broken in *two*.

"You know what? Not so much. I had a year to get ready. And a practice run with Alan, remember."

"Oh, that's *right*!" Straight to the bottom.

"It's okay, Sal. Really. I had a lifetime with someone I loved, in physical form. The fact that she has relinquished that form, shed that space suit, doesn't alter the love I hold for *her*—the astronaut inside the suit. Her energy, and the memories we made on this journey. I believe I'll see her again, experience her again, and that helps. Perhaps in a different form, but her energy lives still. Just not inside a breathing body. At least, that's what I believe, and so that's why I don't seem sad. I *am*, of course, just not in a bad way. I'm not crippled by it."

Pausing a moment, my voice softens. "It's all just a part of life, Sal. The loss. You know that. You chose to adopt Sparkle and Beatrice after Grouper and Tank died. Remember how much that hurt, losing them? Took you years to get over that. But you chose it again anyway. A choice for love means a choice for loss. It just comes with, like grits in the South." I smile. "But the return on that investment is pure joy. Pure joy. Right? So, it's hard to be sad in the midst of that."

Sally looks out the passenger window, her right elbow on the armrest, hand raised to her mouth. Her fingers work her lower lip. We drive in silence a block or two.

She turns from the window to face me. "What do you mean by 'space suit'?" she asks.

I dart a quick glance at her. Her face registers curiosity, yes, but also confusion.

"Well, it's really all about energy, Sal," I begin. "Think of it like this: your bills, your living expenses, and the income you earn cover those. Money comes in every month, and money goes out. Money you generate through efforts expended toward your job. *Your* energy, your physical, intellectual, and emotional energy. You trade your energy and loyalty and skills for cash. That's the bottom line. Money comes *in* your account, money goes *out*." I use one hand to demonstrate a gentle flowing motion, a figure eight.

"It doesn't just disappear, Sal—it goes *elsewhere*, in exchange for other stuff. It alters from one form to another. You know exactly how much is in your account, don't you?" This is a statement, not question. Sally is meticulous and frugal with her money. "And you'd start asking questions if money started mysteriously disappearing, wouldn't you?"

Sally nods. Her eyes reflect understanding and agreement.

"You're trading a lot of energy for anxiety right now, spending a lot of cash on sadness by worrying about what *might* happen with Sparkle. Why waste your money on something so unenjoyable? It's unnecessary and illogical." I shoot her a sidelong smile. "You don't know the future, Sal. None of us do. There's peace in trusting it will turn out alright."

Sally looks out the front windshield and remains quiet, so I continue.

"And maybe, instead of worrying about Sparkle's possible demise you could focus on the time you have with her right now?"

Sally nods, then turns to me and offers a small smile. "Yeah. That sounds good." She cranes her neck, and looks at her precious cat in the carrier on the back seat. "Sound good to you, Miss Sparkle? You want to just go home and play today? That would nice . . ."

Sparkle remains silent. Sally, too. And me.

We stay with our own thoughts the rest of the drive home.

Once we've parked the car exited the elevator on our floor, and after walking Sally and Sparkle to their door, I head a hundred yards down the walkway to my apartment. Stepping inside, I close the door behind me and stand still for a moment. I look around. Everything looks the same, everything is as I left it, in place, neat. There is nothing to clean. There is nothing to do. I'm done. Mary steps forward and pushes Martha aside. I flip an internal switch and shut down.

I take Friday afternoon *off*, spending the rest of the

day in quiet. I don't answer calls or emails. They can wait. I spend the afternoon with Christina, reflecting, and feeling pretty damn good.

The arctic vortex has stiff-armed its way out east after a brutal visit leaving bright sunshine and moderate temperatures. It's lovely to look outside and see blue sky instead of grey clouds and rain.

Fourteen years ago, I succumbed to carbon monoxide poisoning. I was rescued an hour from death. It was a horrid time filled with fear—fear of the present *and* the future. Christina swooped in when I needed her. She helped me heal over the course of the following years. I wrote that story in full in *Threads of Silver*. She helped me find my sense of humor again and taught me how to slow down and notice the subtleties of life, a required prerequisite for appreciation. She helped me adopt a mindset of simplicity. She modeled strength and grace and compassion and helped me believe in my worth and abilities.

And, now, here I sit, finally feeling whole, and at peace, grounded, and grateful, on the very same day Christina left this planet. And she's not here to see it.

But maybe she knows.

I hope so.

I believe so.

That evening I catch a movie on HBO that reminds me of the power of pain and the need to carve a purpose from it in order to move beyond it. In *My Dinner with Hervé*, actor Peter Dinklage plays Hervé Villechaize, the actor who portrayed a character named Tattoo from the 1980s TV show *Fantasy Island*. At the end of the movie (spoiler alert) right before Villechaize kills himself, he says he is "addicted to the fantasy that someone or some-thing can take away the pain of life."

Perhaps we all are. Perhaps in our efforts to assuage whatever pain we might feel—whether emotional or physical—we also thwart our attempts to escape from it. Because the reality is, there is no escaping the pain; there is no love without pain and there is no life without love.

M. Scott Peck, one of my personal heroes, famously opened his seminal book *The Road Less Traveled*—a book which profoundly impacted my interpretation of the word *love* itself—with these words: "Life is difficult," he wrote. "This is a great truth, one of the greatest truths. It is a great truth because once we truly see this truth, we transcend it. Once we truly know that life is difficult— once we truly understand and accept it—then life is no longer difficult. Because once it is accepted, the fact that life is difficult no longer matters."

Embracing the difficult makes it less difficult.

All the planning and preparation, all the details and final instructions, all the well-wishers and caretakers cannot provide protection from the pain of life, particu-larly the pain of the death of those we love, the irrevocable rending, the final scene, the closing curtain. The loss of the comfort provided by our senses—sight, sound, scent and touch— are mourned the most.

But memory is a marvelous monster, our application of it either a help or hinderance as we inch our way through the journey that begins after the goodbyes. *To what shall we say hello?*

We can choose to live *and* die with grace and joy and determination, like Christina, despite the ignorance of our actual expiration date. We can choose quality over quantity, too, in all things.

And we can accept the ultimate paradox, the eternal circular argument that to choose to live demands that we choose to love. Love is the very essence of life, its blood. But choosing love also means choosing loss—one way or the other, sooner or later—because they are two sides of the same coin. It is, like Peck's declaration, an essential and inherent paradox. Finding the balance point within just might be the source of peace.

I was a chaperone once, in my late twenties, for a youth group at the church I attended at the time. I remember sitting in the dining room of the retreat site where we stayed for the weekend and looking through the large doorway to the abutting living room beyond. Around me at the table sat a bunch of rowdy teenagers, eating their dinner and talking over each other. Above the doorjamb—in pretty cursive—someone had hand painted this sentence: *Peace is joy at rest; joy is peace dancing.*

It made an impact on me at that time in my life. It seemed to be a contradiction and I didn't like contradictions back then. I liked black and white and certainty. Back then, I needed external assurances in order for a glimpse of peace to be found but could never seem to find enough to assuage my confusion. I was neither peaceful nor joyful and both states seemed out of reach.

Now, however, I think I'm maybe, almost, sort of beginning to understand. The assurances for which we each search, in our own ways, can only be garnered through the arduous journey of awareness and reflection. Assurances can only be given *by* ourselves, *to* ourselves, *for* ourselves. They are generated from the inside out. I am reminded, once again, of how important it is to pay attention, and to honor our dance with life knowing that death will one day inevitably cut in and take the lead.

When we are willing to put the inescapable pain life brings us to some sort of purpose, we can transform the pain of loss—the very evidence of our humanness—into pearls of wisdom. When we learn to coat our losses, like an oyster does an irritating grain of sand, with a purpose we can create something of great worth and beauty.

And when we string those hard-earned pearls together, and wear them, proudly, with every garment we own, we'll be just like Christina, strutting her stuff, like the thoroughbred she was.

40

STILL THE SAME!

I t's an idle Tuesday in April and I am writing away, thinking about Christina as *Four Fridays* takes early shape. It's a good day. I feel alive. The writing is flowing, and this is not always the case. I am in my comfy bathrobe and fluffy slippers, it's raining, and I don't have to leave my apartment. This makes it a *great* day. On scheduled writing days like this, when opportunity and creativity and execution collide, I'm consumed by it, focused, in a good way, a joyful manner. There's nothing sad about it, despite writing about death and pain and loss. On the contrary, I find the pondering of all those things an enlivening experience. Another paradox.

But I'm stuck on a certain sentence. It is time for a break. So, I stand up, walk around a bit and stretch. I take a deep breath, touch my toes, bounce up and down a few times—get the blood flowing—and return to my seat. And as I do, a song comes on the radio in the background, a song I haven't heard in years—ten years, to be exact. The song is *Do You Realize* by The Flaming Lips.

Had I not taken a break at this precise moment, I

might not have noticed the song when it began to play. When I'm really in flow (of writing), I become impervious to background noises. This tune and its lyrics, however, are hauntingly beautiful, and a strange mixture of affirmation in the midst of loss. I remember *exactly* when and where I heard it for the very first time. It was in 2009, right there in Boca de Tomatlán in the rustic kitchen of the place I rented next door to Christina.

I wept the first time I heard that song. I couldn't explain it, really, why it moved me so deeply. I had arrived in Boca, broken and lost, full of questions, desperate for answers, and the song spoke to me. When I heard its lilting lament—lyrics about realizing that life is fleeting and that everyone you know will someday die, about realizing that it's all just an illusion, even pain—I wept. Hard. I wept face-buried-in-hands hard. I was fresh off my own brush with death and felt completely unmoored, adrift from a life I no longer recognized. So, I cried sad tears, lost tears, and my heart ached in emptiness, because I wanted so badly to realize all those things that the song talked about, but did not, not yet, because I could not. I had not yet lived my way into the answers, into my *own* answers.

Back then, I longed for peace and a pain-free existence and clung to the illusion that certainty and fairness existed, and that I could somehow will both into existence. Now, I realize that peace is a result of accepting the inevitability of pain in life without becoming complacent, pessimistic, or sharp edged as a result.

Sitting in front of my laptop ten years later, in my cozy downtown apartment, the song begins and my heart swells because I no longer cling to the illusion that certainty is soothing or even necessary, or that life and death are separate or contradictory. All is impermanent, save the soul, and even choosing to believe that is a leap of faith. Gratitude is really what matters most as a mechanism, and love is all we take with us when we leave this plane for another. And right now, in this moment, I feel I might burst into a billion bits of joyful light in the abundance of both.

I stop moving, sit down, and become very still. It feels like a wave washing over me, as though Christina is with me right now, singing to me. I close my eyes and listen.

And remember.

I am transported in an instant to a small, barren kitchen, with a ratty old table and a clunky old laptop. I sit, looking out the window over the river to the small town and mountains beyond. I'm writing. And this same song comes on the radio.

Remembering that moment of a decade ago, I can hear the roosters, even now, crowing in Boca's diminishing evening light. I can see Christina through my kitchen window as she comes to the veranda landing on the top level of Casa la Ventana. She leans against the railing, calls my name, and waves me to come join her for a glass of wine. I lean back in my rickety wood chair, turn toward her through the kitchen doorway and wave back. I can see her clearly, in vivid detail; her short blond hair, long tan legs, broad, bright smile. Mattie is there with her tail wagging. Silvia comes into view and waves. *Those remembered live forever.*

The song ends and I open my eyes in real time in Toronto. I wipe tears from my cheeks and smile.

My friend did not *die*. She lives somewhere, s0mehow. She changed states, that's all. When I suspend the limits of physical sensations and employ the memory machine, she's right here, right now, playing with me, communicating through the radio, thrilled that I'm paying attention once again, and that when I close my eyes, I can hear and see her and feel her.

And you know what?

She looks exactly the same.

EPILOGUE

Christina left detailed instructions concerning her exit. She was clear and precise until the end. There would be no casket for her. She wanted to be cremated and her ashes distributed in four distinct places.

In February, one portion was buried in her Gramma Garden beneath all her cherished orchids. Christina is now a permanent part of her beloved garden.

The next week, Joy, Nate, Karen, and their eldest son, Kade, along with Amauri, Toto, Isabel, and others, hiked with a guide to the top of the east mountain to pay homage to Palma Sola. It is an arduous journey. Jaguars live there. As Joy remarked afterwards, "Man! The things we do for love!" Under the shade of her precious palm tree growing at the top of the mountain, strong and solitary, they placed a portion of Christina's remains along with a bottle of Casa la Ventana Tequila, a favorite cameo necklace, and a joint. She will forever overlook her beloved Boca.

In June, a portion of her was sprinkled into the ocean in the town's annual celebration of Mariner's Day.

The locals get drunk, get in their boats, lay giant wreaths of flowers in the water, and remember those lost at sea. Christina enjoyed Mariner's Day celebrations, and her floral wreath was particularly grand and beautiful. She is now a part of the ocean, too.

Finally, she wanted a portion of her remains to be buried at the Botanical Gardens of Puerto Vallarta, a sprawling, natural exhibit of indigenous plant and tree growth that Christina supported. She brought her B&B guests there regularly, always offering more than people paid for. She gave a lot of herself. People gathered there on November 16th for her final celebration of life. Unable to attend myself, Joy reported that it was a wonderful testimonial, the culmination of a remarkable life.

Leo had his operation on February 24th, as scheduled, and it went well, as hoped. He returned home with short-term care, as planned. Leo is nothing if not precise in his assessment of, and entrance into, a future reality he wants to create.

Leo is a walking paradox. With a new hip.

Isabel, the housekeeper, still takes care of Casa la Ventana as she studies to become a real estate agent, and Toto continues to care for the grounds and gardens.

Bella went to live with Nate and Karen and their boys in Seattle. Joy tells me she was happy to go and has acclimated overnight to her new home. Bella knew. Her rescuer, her goddess, was gone, and it was time for a new family. Dogs are better than people about things like that.

The big surprise was Maya, who most of us thought would decline rapidly after Christina died, but didn't. Don wanted her, she seemed to want to go with him, and so they now live in his little apartment and, by all accounts, are flourishing. Maya has given Don a reason to get up and walk, and a pair of ears that listen without interruption, correction, or addition. Maya gets a lot of loving from Don and that's making him a bit better, too.

Bruja stayed at Casa la Ventana. Like my landlord's dog Mattie at my old *casa* next door, she now comes with the place. And, I suspect, from now on, so will Christina's spirit.

And so does Joy, who has agreed to stay on during high season each year to oversee the place, as long as her dogs come too. Because, as I could have predicted, she adopted a street dog the week after Christina died, quite by mistake, she says, but I suspect it's no coincidence that she returned to Colorado Springs with a living, breathing reminder of Boca. She's brought a bit of her Mexican momma back with her.

Kim's dog passed. Sally's cat didn't. And Peyton is toilet trained.

And me? I spent the year since Christina's death writing this book, as a way to process my grief, as well as to honor her life, her death, and our friendship. The themes of pain, purpose, and peace emerged as I wrote, and I often felt Christina's presence nearby as I typed. I printed the 11:11 picture and framed it in a shadow frame, the only one in my home. It hangs in my bedroom and I smile each time I pass it. Though I shall miss her until I take a seat beside her to watch what I hope will be my own merry Meryl life review, I am at peace. And so, so grateful to have known and loved her.

Cynthia *Mary* Cook (Rice) Barlow
February 1, 2020

∾

11:11

Even in our sleep, pain which cannot forget
   Falls drop by drop upon the heart,
   Until, in our despair,
   Against our will,
   Comes Wisdom
   Through the awful grace of God.

AESCHYLUS

ACKNOWLEDGMENTS

All the names in *Four Fridays* are real save Paul and Ruby and their children, pseudonyms for the grieving couple I met on my fourth and final Friday with Christina. My special thanks to Joy, Isabel, Toto, Alesia, and many others for the love and care they extended towards Christina while she lived. They are earth angels.

I have been fortunate to have a lot of people in my corner for a lot of years, more than I can recount here. You know who you are. My humble thanks. Several helped me enormously as *Four Fridays* took shape, and I'd like to acknowledge them by name.

To brilliant authors Maureen Fisher and Karen M. Black, whose early input awakened me to the need for back story and perspective, and sent me into a two-month bout of complete paralysis, thank goodness for your courage. I love you both. For your support, and encouragement (over twenty years), I am eternally grateful.

To Tara Tosh Kennedy, whose creative eye read the revised version once paralysis lifted. You are a delight whose presence reminds me of wild rabbits dancing in the moonlight.

To Michael Rice, artist, and wicked-good writer, who not only listened to his mother read the manuscript aloud but also word-smithed the book summary sentences—something I am apparently wicked-lousy at. You are a bright light in my life. You remind me, over and over, that the only thing that really matters is love, and a good dog to greet you.

To Kim and Sally for their friendship, and trusting me to share glimpses into their lives.

And to my editor and publishers, John and Boni Wagner-Stafford, and all the folks at Ingenium Books—particularly Denise Willson and her expert proofreading skills—your early enthusiasm and guidance through this project made all the difference in bringing *Four Fridays* to fruition. Thank you for the gift of your expertise.

And, finally, to Christina, whose life, love, and light continue to inspire me daily, I thank you for being you.

Christina and me in Boca, 2014.
I'm wearing the earrings I had forgotten she gave me in 2009.
Can you hear the Universe laughing?

Joy, Leo and Cynthia 2011

Joy and Toto 2018

Christina and Isabel 2016

Alesia and Joy

Maya and Bella 2019
Bruja's somewhere sleeping in the sun

Casa la Ventana

The mountain view from Christina's eastern balcony

The second half of the endless staircase

ABOUT THE AUTHOR

Cynthia Barlow is a facilitator, coach and author of several books. A specialist in Emotional Intelligence, she has conducted leadership development programs for over thirty years for clients like TD Bank, Bell, Bank of America, AutoZone and Amex. Her coaching clients range from top executives to everyday people looking for ways to notch up their performance.

Photo by Michelle Valberg, Valberg Imaging

A popular and experienced key-note speaker, Cynthia has inspired thousands of people to look a little deeper and reach a little higher with her direct, humorous, and slightly sassy style. She says the highest compliment she has ever received is this: "You paint word-pictures blind people can see."

Mother to two grown sons (and two grandchildren), Cynthia is passionate about words, water, puppies, and chocolate, which she is certain is a valid food group.

She is driven by truth, trust, and transparency, and makes her home in Toronto.

IF YOU ENJOYED FOUR FRIDAYS

If you enjoyed *Four Fridays*, in honor of Christina and her legacy, I would greatly appreciate you taking the time to post a positive review where you bought or obtained this book.

Here is a link you can use that will take you directly to the Four Fridays review page on Amazon, for example:

https://ingeniumbooks.com/FFReview

And maybe tell your friends. Or gift them a copy. Or both. You get the idea. Because the world could use more Christinas. My heartfelt thanks in advance.

A portion of profits from the sale of *Four Fridays* will go towards Christina's philanthropic efforts by helping to fund the *Becas* Scholarship program as well as the Boca Medical and Dental Clinic.

I post a weekly blog every Monday morning and have for over a decade. My posts are a way to begin your week on an upbeat, thoughtful note. People seem to like it. You can find it on my website, www.C3Conversations.com. It's free.

ALSO BY CYNTHIA BARLOW

Threads Of Silver: A Five Year Search for Simplicity, Sunshine, and a Fresh Start

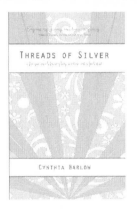

Resilience: It's Not About Bouncing Back

How Deep is Today? A Bedtime Story for Grown-ups

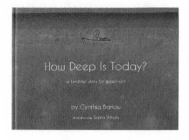

Made in the USA
Monee, IL
10 May 2020

30547729R00180